ORTHO'S All About

Vines
and Climbers

Written by R. William Thomas

Meredith® Books
Des Moines, Iowa

Ortho® Books
An imprint of Meredith® Books

Ortho's All About Vines and Climbers
Editor: Michael McKinley
Art Director: Tom Wegner
Copy Chief: Catherine Hamrick
Copy and Production Editor: Terri Fredrickson
Contributing Copy Editors: Chardel Gibson Blaine,
    Deborah Gibson, Martin Miller
Technical Consultants: Harrison L. Flint, Michael A. Dirr
Contributing Proofreaders: Kathy Eastman,
    Colleen Johnson, Mary Pas
Contributing Designer: Tim Abramowitz
Contributing Illustrator: Cyndie Wooley
Contributing Map Illustrator: Jana Fothergill
Contributing Prop/Photo Stylists: Mary E. Klingaman,
    Pamela K. Peirce
Indexer: Donald Glassman
Electronic Production Coordinator: Paula Forest
Editorial and Design Assistants: Kathleen Stevens,
    Karen Schirm
Production Director: Douglas M. Johnston
Production Manager: Pam Kvitne
Assistant Prepress Manager: Marjorie J. Schenkelberg

**Additional Editorial Contributions from
    Art Rep Services**
Director: Chip Nadeau
Designers: lk Design, Shawn Wallace
Illustrators: Carolyn A. Cohen, John Teisberg

Meredith® Books
Editor in Chief: James D. Blume
Design Director: Matt Strelecki
Managing Editor: Gregory H. Kayko
Executive Ortho Editor: Benjamin W. Allen

Director, Sales & Marketing, Retail: Michael A. Peterson
Director, Sales & Marketing, Special Markets:
    Rita McMullen
Director, Sales & Marketing, Home & Garden Center
    Channel: Ray Wolf
Director, Operations: George A. Susral

Vice President, General Manager: Jamie L. Martin

Meredith Publishing Group
President, Publishing Group: Christopher M. Little
Vice President, Consumer Marketing & Development:
    Hal Oringer

Meredith Corporation
Chairman and Chief Executive Officer: William T. Kerr
Chairman of the Executive Committee: E.T. Meredith III

On the cover: Morning glory 'Heavenly Blue' is a favorite
annual vine for nearly instant effect and lavish blue
flowers. Photograph by Maggie Oster.

All of us at Ortho® Books are dedicated to providing you
with the information and ideas you need to enhance your
home and garden. We welcome your comments and
suggestions about this book. Write to us at:
    Meredith Corporation
    Ortho Books
    1716 Locust St.
    Des Moines, IA 50309–3023

If you would like more information on other Ortho
products, call 800-225-2883 or visit us at www.ortho.com

Photographers:
(Some photographers credited retain copyright © to the listed
photographs.) T = top, C = center, B = bottom, R = right, L = left.
William D. Adams: 76TL; **L. Albee:** 17BL, 72BL; **Patricia J.
Bruno/Positive Images:** 6TL, 15TR, 51TR, 58BL; **John E. Bryan:** 71C;
Les Campbell/Positive Images: 17TL; **Walter Chandoha:** 58CLB;
Crandall & Crandall: 17BR, 44C, 79CR; **R. Todd Davis:** 5BR, 22BL;
Joseph DeSciose: 78BR ; **Alan L. Detrick:** 11BR, 32TL, 85 Row 2-2,
85 Row 4-1; **Alan & Linda Detrick:** 45CR, 55BL inset, 82BR, 84 Row
3-1 & 2, 85 Row 3-2, 88TRB; **Thomas E. Eltzroth:** 48TL, 56TL, 81TR,
90BR; **Catriona Tudor Erler:** 85 Row 3-1; **Derek Fell:** 20BL, 29CR,
31BL, 36TL, 38TR, 48BR, 55CR, 58TL, 58CLT, 61 Row 4-1, 62CL,
64CL, 65TR, 66TL, 70BL, 71CR, 72CR, 83CR, 84 Row 4-1, 86T, 86C,
91TR; **Charles Marden Fitch:** 62TL, 67 Row 3-2, 84 Row 1-3, 85 Row
4-2; **Harrison L. Flint:** 19TL, 25TR, 28TL, 49B ,77BR; **Jack
Foley/Positive Images:** 20TL; **John Glover:** 6CL, 10TL, 11BL, 12CLB,
17CL, 18BL, 20CR, 23TR, 24TLR, 25BL, 27CR, 29BR, 33TR, 44TR,
59 Row 1-1, 59 Row 2-2, 59 Row 2-4, 60TL, 60BL, 61 Row 3-1, 67 Row
1-1, 67 Row 3-1 & 4, 73C, CR, BL, BC, BR, 75TC, 79TR, 84 Row 1-2,
84 Row 2-1, 87TR, 88BL, 89BL, 89BC, 89BR; **David Goldberg:** 40 all,
41 all, 42 all, 43 all, 44BL, 44CR, 45TR, 45CL,90 BL; **Mick Hales:**
55TR; **Harry Haralambou:** 8TL & BL, 14TL, 17TR, 21BR, 83T, 84
Row 1-1; **Harry Haralambou/Positive Images:** 17CR, 19C, 37BL;
Pamela J. Harper: 4BR, 7BR, 18BR, 23BR, 24TLC, 29BL, 32CL, 44TL,
56CL, 65BR, 67 Row 3-3, 67 Row 4-4, 69BRC & BRB, 70TL, 74TL;
Jerry Harpur: 4CL, 16BR, 29TR, 57CR, 62BL, 89TR, 91BL; **Jessie M.
Harris:** 63T, 85 Row 3-3; **Lynne Harrison:** 26C, 33BR; **Jerry
Howard/Positive Images:** 13TR, 16TL; **Bill Johnson:** 36BR, 71BL,
75TR, 85 Row 4-3; **Dency Kane:** 11CL, 38BL, 45TL, 59 Row 4-1,
68BLT, 69BRT, 84 Row 2-2, 84 Row 3-3; **Mark Kane:** 49T; **Lynn
Karlin:** 30TL, 30CL; **Michael Landis:** 45BR; **Andrew Lawson:** 25BRC,
59 Row 1-3, 59 Row 2-3, 59 Row 3-1, 59 Row 3-4, 66BL, 67 Row 1-2, 1-
3 & 1-4, 67 Row 2-1 & 2-2, 75CR, 81BR, 85 Row 1-1 & 1-2, 87B inset;
Lee Lockwood/Positive Images: 12TL, 15BR; **Kathy Longinaker:**
47BR; **Janet Loughery:** 61 Row 2-2, 61 Row 3-2; **Allan Mandell:** 11TR,
59 Row 1-4, 59 Row 3-2 & 3-3, 59 Row 4-3 & 4-4, 61 Row 2-3; **Charles
Mann:** 14BL, 18T, 21TR, 36CL, 61 Row 1-1, 73TR; **Marilynn McAra:**
15CR, 71BC; **Bryan McCay:** 44BR, 46BR, 47TR, 47CR; **David
McDonald/PhotoGarden:** 5CR, 6BR, 9T, 25CR, 37TR, 52L, 59 Row 1-
2, 59 Row 2-1, 61 Row 1-2, 61 Row 4-2, 68TL, 88TRC; **Michael
McKinley:** 22TL, 39TL; **Clive Nichols:** 53B, 67 Row 2-4, 75C, 78TL,
79BL, 88B inset; **Clive Nichols/Mrs. Glaisher, Hildenborough, Kent:**
52R; **Clive Nichols/Pyrford Court, Surrey:** 89TC; **Maggie Oster:**
21CL, 29TC, 31TR, 39TC, 69TR, 71TR, 71CL, 77TR, 80TLBL, 90TL;
Jerry Pavia: 16BL, 24TLL, 37CL, 39BR, 44TC, 56BL, 64BR, 83BR, 84
Row 4-2, 86BR, 88TL; **Graham Rice/New Leaf Images:** 24C, 88TRT;
Cheryl R. Richter: 9BR; **Field Roebuck:** 85 Row 1-3; **Susan A. Roth:**
6BL, 27TR, 36BL, 39TR, 39BL, 53CR, 55BR, 61 Row 1-3, 63BR, 67
Row 4-1, 2, & 3, 71BR, 75TL, 78BL, 78CR, 80TLBR, 80B inset, 82TL,
87CR; **Richard Shiell:** 26L, 33CR, 38TC, 38BR, 39BC, 53TR, 54TL,
57TR, 57BR, 61 Row 2-1, 61 Row 3-3, 61 Row 4-3, 63B inset, 67 Row
2-3, 72TL, 75CL, BR, 76BL, 80TLTL & TLTR, 82BL, 84 Row 4-3,
86BL, 87BR, 91BC & BR; **Pam Spaulding/Positive Images:** 29CL,
83BL; **Albert Squillace/Positive Images:** 85 Row 2-3; **Sabina Mueller
Sulgrove:** 13CL, 23BL, 25CL, 32BL, 66CL; **Michael S. Thompson:**
19BL, 22BR, 24BL, 25BRB, 26R, 27TL, 28BL, 36CR, 38TL, 38BC,
46TL, 46BL, 59 Row 4-2, 63CR, 64TL, 65BL, 70TL inset, 73CL, 79BR,
82TR, 84 Row 2-3, 85 Row 2-1; **Mark Turner:** 10CL, 13BR, 68BLB,
80BL; **judywhite/New Leaf Images:** 19BR

Ortho Books acknowledges the following for technical assistance in
the writing of this book: Marty Kromer, Tres Fromme, Colvin
Randall, Richard Bitner, Sharol Schwass, and Rosemary Sack-Inslee

Note to the Readers: Due to differing conditions, tools,
and individual skills, Meredith Corporation assumes no
responsibility for any damages, injuries suffered, or losses
incurred as a result of following the information published
in this book. Before beginning any project, review the
instructions carefully, and if any doubts or questions remain,
consult local experts or authorities. Because codes and
regulations vary greatly, you always should check with
authorities to ensure that your project complies with all
applicable local codes and regulations. Always read and observe
all of the safety precautions provided by manufacturers of any
tools, equipment, or supplies,
and follow all accepted safety procedures.

THE VERSATILITY OF
VINES

Nothing bursts across an autumn landscape like the vibrant oranges and reds of the crimson glory vine, which grows up to 20 feet per season.

Vines are amazing plants. In the wild they scramble over rocks and wind themselves through brush and other plants. They climb the trunks of trees and reach for light. They arch over streams and sprawl through woodland meadows. They plunge from cliffs. They are the cloth of nature's landscape and take the form of things they cover. And because of their frequently rapid growth and unique ability to cloak and drape—often with showy color—vines play a host of unique roles in the garden.

The specialized method a vine uses to climb is important to know because it determines the kind of structure we can grow it on. *Twiners*, like morning glory and wisteria, wrap their stems around supports and will grow on posts, chain link, and lattices. Vines that climb by *tendrils*, such as sweet pea and passionflower, reach out and curl threadlike extensions of branch or leaf around netting or the stems of shrubs. Vines that grow with clinging *rootlets*, such as creeping fig and climbing hydrangea, attach themselves to masonry, tree trunks, or rocks with small roots or adhesivelike pads. *Climbers* and *sprawlers*, such as rambling roses, do not climb readily by themselves, but their long, arching, sprawling stems can be tied to lattice or frameworks anchored in walls or other structures, and achieve often amazing heights.

As with many other plants, there are both annual and perennial vines. Annual vines live for less than a year (sometimes only a single season), but their quick growth offers you "instant" color and design—and their short life span means you can change their effect from year to year. Perennials live far longer than a year and can become the fixtures that are permanent in your design. Some perennials are herbaceous; they die to the ground each winter and regrow quickly in the spring. Others, called "woody" vines, retain aboveground growth all winter. Some woody vines keep their leaves all winter (evergreens). Others lose their leaves each fall (deciduous).

Because they are thin, with flexible stems, and because they usually grow rapidly—up, not out—vines have an edge over trees, shrubs, and flowers in designing your garden space or landscape. They are easy to grow, affordable, and forgiving of injury.

Vines offer a wonderful range of color, texture, and fragrance. They can match, complement, or contrast other plants and structures in your outdoor environment. They will moderate light, wind, and temperature. Some will even provide delicious fruit!

As you read the following pages of this book, you'll find just the information you need to make vines your partners in design.

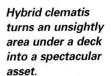

Freestanding arches, arbors, and pergolas can set off garden areas and create a sense of enclosure and privacy.

Hybrid clematis turns an unsightly area under a deck into a spectacular asset.

Utilitarian structures such as chain link fences become bold areas of color and solid dividers of space when covered with vines, such as this cross vine.

SET THE STAGE

Vines on the west and south sides of a house can lower the temperature of the wall and reduce cooling costs inside. Plant directly on your home as was done with this Boston ivy, or use arbors, lattice, or netting over the wall for training vines.

Quick shade comes with a vine such as this wisteria over a patio. Plant the vine at the edge of the paving and train it over an arbor or other structure for attractive cooling in summer sitting areas.

A trumpet vine shades a hammock.

All plants can have a positive effect on your outdoor world, but vines are special. Because of the way they grow, they work wonders where other plants fail.

Take advantage of their unique character. They can help you get out of the house and into the landscape—a landscape they've made more livable.

SUN, WIND, AND SOUND SCREENS

Filter sun to help cool your home in summer. A vine on the west or south wall cools with its shade. A cool porch—especially one that faces west—can mean the difference between getting outside in the evening or staying cooped up indoors. Shade it with vines that climb on wires. You can attach them top and bottom with hooks or eyes.

Vines can shade the outdoors, too. In new home lawns, where there are no trees or only saplings, you don't have to wait for trees to grow. Vines on a latticework can make shade even in small backyards. Arbors with their shaded tops and open sides provide breezy dappled spots or freshen the corners of your garden. Vines can block the wind—even in the winter. An evergreen trellis can make the winter morning walk to the garage just a bit more comfortable in a bitter wind, and a vine-covered arbor on the windy side makes a winter garden warmer.

This small trellis shades a bench for pleasant summertime sitting.

If you would like a quieter retreat, vines, especially ones with large, soft leaves, soften sounds that would otherwise bounce off hard surfaces.

FRESHEN THE AIR

If you've ever walked in the summer sun from an open space into a grove of trees, you've noticed the air is instantly cooler. Vines, like all plants, add oxygen, absorb carbon dioxide, filter dust, and reduce pollution. Oxygen makes air pure, fresher, and more pleasant to breathe. Vines, however, grow where other plants will not, and they can be natural air fresheners in landscape spaces you might not use—even in cramped urban areas. And by careful placement of vines that have fragrant flowers, they'll mask odors, too.

REDUCE EROSION

Some vines grow horizontally along the ground as successfully as others scramble up trees and supports. These ground-huggers are ideal for slopes that need stabilizing. Virginia creeper and English ivy will cover areas quickly and thickly. Virginia creeper gives you the added benefit of lush red fall color, and English ivy is evergreen. Both root where stems touch the soil, so they multiply as they grow, a real advantage when the slope is very rocky and digging is difficult. They tolerate drought and do equally well in sun or shade, making them great survivors on dry locations. In the South, use maypops and Confederate jasmine on such slopes.

ATTRACT BIRDS

Birds will love you for your vines. Their increased presence will be a surprising benefit. Vines offer safe shelter for many species of birds and nectar for others. Robins specifically seem to like nesting within the branches of vines, and hummingbirds may hover in the blooms of flowering varieties. Vines on the house will bring birds close to your living areas, maybe within view of a window. Evergreen vines will be perches for overwintering birds at night and will provide cover during the day.

Ground-hugging vines like variegated wintercreeper do not need much soil to thrive. Plant small vines amidst rocks on a slope. As the vines grow, they will root repeatedly, blanketing the slope.

QUICK SHADE FOR PAVED AREAS

Vines make great shade plants for carports, patios, and even cabanas over sitting areas. Build a simple arbor or other structure over a paved area and train a vine to climb up and provide shade. Make sure the structure is strong enough to support the weight. Plant at the edge of the paving, or if that is not possible, plant it in a large container set on the pavement. American wisteria, akebia, Carolina jessamine, and hops do well in such situations, as does the silver lace vine shown above.

Avoid vines with large flowers or fruit; they will shower debris from above. Trumpet vines, Asian wisterias, and grapes are among the messiest.

ROOMS WITH A VIEW

A transparent wall formed by post and chain is covered by roses. This gives a sense of enclosure to the garden without the wall creating a solid barrier. Views are allowed into the surrounding landscape.

Create the best of both worlds with vine ceilings. These structures help you escape the intensity of summer sun and heat, while providing friends and neighbors a welcoming front row seat to your garden's beauty.

Oddly enough, space is "defined" only when something puts an end to it. Think of a room in your home, for instance. The space in it is defined by its walls, the ceiling, and the floor. There are views to the outside through its windows, views that can be muted with shades, cut off entirely by blinds and drapery, or made transparent with curtains.

Now take yourself outdoors and take your idea of "room" with you. You can create rooms right here in your landscape, and vines can define their space: They can be the ceilings and the floors, and the walls—complete with windows. But it's the walls of this room that vines create most readily.

OUTDOOR ROOMS

You can start with only a suggestion of a wall—a single post and a twining vine. Combine two posts with chain between them and create a transparent wall with roses. It gives a sense of enclosure and still lets you look beyond into the garden or surrounding landscape. A vine-covered arbor or trelliswork at the end of your garden can make its own seclusion, and even though this living wall *seems* solid, its texture is more gentle than a hard-surface wall or wooden fence.

An open front yard may seem friendly to the street, but it is not very conducive to lounging or entertaining because there is a lack of privacy. Enclose the space with a vine-covered fence or arbor and the area feels more like "your space."

Views from one part of the yard may be totally open, framed by vines on vines or vines on structures, partially closed by uncovered fences, or totally blocked.

Shrubs, of course, and hedges, fences, and built walls can also create garden rooms. But what makes vines unique is their ability to form a thin and living wall, one that is quickly established and inexpensively shaped, is flexible and easily modified, comes in an array of colors—and never needs painting.

ADD HEIGHT

Creating boundaries with vines also adds vertical design elements to an otherwise flat landscape. They do that without "getting in the way." Vine-covered posts enclose an area and keep open the view beyond. Tripods in a

An arbor circling a yard encloses the space, provides a background, and invites you in. Arbors are especially welcoming on hot days because they offer a cool respite from the sun.

vegetable or perennial garden give structure, height, and a feeling of mass.

A single vine-covered structure can center the view. Repeated patterns can punctuate the openness of your garden and give it rhythm, and depending on your choice of vines, a sense of mystery or the gentle motion of the light.

KIDS' SPACE

Annual vines grown on simple net structures make enticing and fun outdoor playrooms. There is an almost endless variety of possible shapes because vines are "plastic" and take on the form of whatever they cover. Begin by setting posts or poles to outline the structure you want. Cover the posts with string or wire netting (available at hardware stores and garden centers). Try four-sided boxes, teepees, wigwams, tunnels, or tents. If a sufficient number of arching poles is used, as with a wigwam or tunnel, netting may not even be necessary.

Once the structure is made, plant an annual vine because it will cover the structure quickly, have interesting flowers and/or fruit, and can be changed each year. Ornamental gourds, scarlet runner beans, and nasturtiums are a few possibilities. Have the children plant vining vegetables, such as cucumbers and lima beans. They will take pride in growing the plants (and may even be enticed to eat the vegetables). If the structure is large enough, plant more than one type of vine. Avoid poisonous vines or floriferous ones that may attract bees.

Annual vines need a lot of light and hot weather to grow well. Don't plant them until all danger of frost is past and the days and nights are reliably warm. Plant seeds in place or start them inside about four weeks before the last chance of frost. You can then transplant them to the playhouse structure.

A playhouse teepee covered with beans.

HIDE AND SCREEN

Hide something unattractive with a covering of vines. Above, a doghouse is covered with nasturtiums, and at right, a stump is covered with Jackman clematis.

VINES FOR SCREENS

EVERGREEN VINES
English ivy (*Hedera helix*)
Persian ivy (*Hedera colchica*)
Wintercreeper (*Euonymus fortunei*)
Creeping fig (*Ficus pumila*)
Carolina jessamine (*Gelsemium sempervirens*)
Evergreen clematis (*Clematis armandii*)
Cross vine (*Bignonia capreolata*)
Confederate jasmine (*Trachelospermum jasminoides*)

RAPID GROWERS
Morning glories (*Ipomoea*)
Virginia creeper (*Parthenocissus quinquefolia*)
Cup-and-saucer vine (*Cobaea scandens*)
English ivy (*Hedera helix*)
Akebia (*Akebia quinata*)
Wisteria (*Wisteria*)
Dutchman's pipe (*Aristolochia macrophylla*)
Beans (*Dolichos, Phaseolus*)
Potato vine (*Solanum jasminoides*)
Moonflower (*Ipomoea alba*)
Trumpet vine (*Campsis radicans*)

Just as you might use a slipcover to give an old chair a new look, you can use vines as a "fabric" in your landscape to cover up its blemishes. By choosing an attractive vine you can even turn an eyesore into a beautiful focal point.

HIDE

A garden shed is extremely useful in a cluttered world, but it is rarely attractive. Its colors may clash, and it probably never looked like it belonged in the garden. Now it can: Drape it with poultry netting and plant English ivy for an evergreen cover. Sweet autumn clematis will bring late summer flowers and fragrance.

Dog pens and runs may be a necessity, but are not pretty spots. Cover the fence with foliage, or better yet, with a vine that flowers. Annual morning glories are quick and pretty.

Anemone clematis is vigorous, and its blooms are vanilla-scented in the spring.

Concrete block is a quick and easy way to build a wall, but give it color and texture; cover it with a vine that clings with rootlets. Climbing hydrangea or a false climbing hydrangea will reward you with a great show of flowers each spring. Boston ivy produces a tight, green covering over the wall and becomes brilliantly colored in the autumn. Wintercreeper and creeping fig are evergreens that can also be ground covers if there is room in front of the wall.

Deck posts can be elegant columns; transform them with Dutchman's pipe or climbing roses. Plant moonflower, and your deck will become a fragrant evening retreat.

The beauty of using vines is that they not only cover those unsightly objects, they become pleasant distractions. Make an eyesore a focal point with climbing roses, honeysuckle, and any of the annual vines that will produce color throughout the summer.

SCREEN OUT

House too close to a road? Neighbor have different tastes than yours? Live near a commercial area? Temporary quarters? The solution is simple, inexpensive, and takes up almost no space. Erect a rapid screen with wire mesh fencing and grow a tendril vine. A latticework with hyacinth bean on it will be quickly covered with pink flowers and purple pods. Or transform your existing chain-link fence into an attractive living wall that screens your view. Choose a vine that grows quickly, and you will be enjoying that screen by summer. Evergreen vines tend to be a bit slower but offer year-long cover.

SCREEN IN

As screens, vines do double duty. In addition to hiding something you don't want to see, they add privacy to a garden by blocking the view from the outside. If you want less of your yard to be visible from the street, a neighbor's yard, or a commercial area, solve the problem with a screen of vines.

Cover eyesores or screen an ugly view with a vine. Clockwise from top left: cover a rock pile with Emerald Gaiety wintercreeper. Screen an ugly view with a hedge of climbing roses. Create a secluded nook with the rose 'Tausendschon'. Provide front-gate privacy with a generous, beautiful face to the street using Ville de Lyon clematis.

NOOKS AND CRANNIES

Vines use little space and are perfect for small gardens. Most are only inches wide yet provide a natural element in an otherwise artificial environment. Flowering vines add color to bare walls and extend the garden skyward but don't reduce space for relaxing and entertaining.

English ivy cascades exuberantly out of a window box.

VINES FOR SMALL PLACES

Kolomikta vine (*Actinidia kolomikta*)
Climbing snapdragon (*Asarina scandens*)
Hybrid clematis (*Clematis*)
Climbing bleeding heart (*Dicentra scandens*)
Hyacinth bean (*Dolichos lablab*)
Climbing hydrangea (*Hydrangea petiolaris*)
Sweet pea (*Lathyrus odoratus*)
Yellow honeysuckle (*Lonicera flava*)
Trumpet honeysuckle (*Lonicera sempervirens*)
Scarlet runner bean (*Phaseolus coccincus*)
Purple bell vine (*Rhodochiton atrosanguineus*)
Climbing miniature roses (*Rosa*)
False climbing hydrangea (*Schizophragma hydrangeoides*)

In most small gardens, after planting your favorite shrubs and flowers, the only place to go is up. Vines are perfect vertical features for small garden areas since, if chosen correctly, they take up little ground space.

Vines bring a touch of green or an extra flush of bloom to small gardens and balconies. They take the garden skyward, create privacy, and block unattractive views.

In apartment settings and small urban yards where there is no open ground in which to plant, vines are perfect in containers. Many thrive in pots and bring lush foliage and textural interest not only to balconies but to paved areas and decks as well.

TOWNHOUSE AND CITY GARDENS

Urban gardens are often surrounded by walls. Vines pull the garden upward yet do not take up space needed for seating and dining. Trees, of course, do that, too, but they occupy precious space and their roots make it difficult to grow other plants. If it's shade you need, build an arbor or pergola for silver lace vine or ornamental gourds. If light is at a premium, vines on the walls soften large expanses of masonry without increasing shade.

Townhouse owners often face the challenge of having little privacy or sense of enclosure. Hedges will give you privacy but only in return for regular pruning, and they devour valuable space. Vines, trained on netting or fences, are only inches wide; they create privacy without sacrificing land. If you need ground-level screening of a neighbor's second-floor windows, an arbor or latticework can provide it.

DECKS, ROOFTOPS, AND BALCONIES

Before growing any plants in containers above ground, there are things you need to keep in mind. Make sure your structure is strong enough to support the pot. Choose vines that don't become too large. (*See the box at left for suggestions.*) Containers on balconies and rooftops need trays underneath to catch irrigation water. You will not win praise from your neighbors if your vines drip on their balconies.

Balcony gardens are always tight on space because of the limited size of the available area and the weight limits of the structure. Even small trees are likely to be too large and heavy. Vines are the ideal solution; they add a sense of the vertical without taking up too much space or added weight.

VINES IN CONTAINERS

Before you plant in containers, ask yourself these few questions. Will the container be permanent or will you move it? How will the vine climb? Can the container survive freezing and thawing? What will the container, plant, and climbing structure look like in winter?

Permanent containers remain in place year-round. They become an island on a deck, balcony, or paved area, so they need to be attractive every day. Movable containers are more flexible. Try growing a sun-loving vine in a sunny spot to encourage blooming and then move it into a shady sitting area for color.

Large terra-cotta pots offer plenty of root space for a climber such as Alice du Pont mandevilla, as well as for companion plants. Terra-cotta does not tolerate much freezing and thawing and is best brought inside for the winter.

Whiskey barrels and other wooden planters survive well in all types of weather. If building your own, choose a rot-resistant wood, such as pressure-treated lumber, cypress, cedar, or plantation-grown teak.

Balance your need for portability with size; large containers offer more root space than small ones and require less frequent watering.

Climbing vines need appropriate supports to hold them. Annual climbers are replanted each year and don't require a long-lasting structure, but perennial vines need something permanent. For twining vines, such as honeysuckle, a simple bamboo pole works well. The base will rot every two years or so, but you can push it farther into the soil or place a new one next to the old one and the vine will soon attach to it. The old pole can remain.

A small lattice structure or netting stretched between posts or attached by hooks to a wall works well for tendril vines, such as clematis. The structure doesn't actually need to be in the container. A nearby wall (for rootlet vines, such as hydrangea or Virginia creeper) or netting set up along the edge of the balcony or hard surface can provide the necessary support.

Some vines are cascaders. They help hide the container and soften its lines. English ivy, sweet potato vine, wintercreeper, climbing hydrangea, and false climbing hydrangea are all excellent.

Winter brings other challenges. Freezing and thawing cracks and destroys most terra-cotta (clay), but fiberglass, wood, and concrete tolerate winter well.

Consider how the vine, support, and container look in winter. Using glazed pots and painted lattice makes groupings more interesting in the dormant season. With an evergreen variety, you won't have to worry about how the container looks. Try an evergreen vine, such as English ivy or wintercreeper. They offer cultivars with yellow or purple leaves, as well as green.

A permanent planter is a garden oasis in a desert of paving.

THE VINE ARTS

Frame a view with a vine.

Frame an object with a vine.

Vines are more than functional. They, like no other member of the plant world, can take you on an endless journey of design. They can frame views or objects. They can be focal points or provide unity and repetition of form, line, color, and texture. They can quiet a garden setting or bring it alive with brightness. They can be small points of interest or major backdrops for other plantings. Many vines can cover large expanses with relative ease. Others are restrained and can be tucked away in uncommon places.

FRAME THE VIEW

A frame guides the eye and adds a sense of mystery. Try growing Boston ivy or cross vine around a window in a masonry wall. On a wood or vinyl-sided wall, build a lattice or surround the window with netting for climbers. Place a bamboo pole next to a low window and let a twiner grow to eye-level. Arch a Dutchman's pipe across the window. When it blooms, you'll have a great view of delightful, but usually overlooked, flowers.

A lone, plain bench is not terribly welcoming; it's isolated and exposed. Frame or surround the sides of the bench with vines and it becomes a beautiful, comfortable, and private retreat. The shade will make it a cooler place to lounge, rest, or read.

An archway makes you want to peer through it; it frames the view beyond and is a transition into the garden. A sculpture, small fountain, gazing ball, or special plant within or just beyond the arch adds depth and highlights the view.

FOCAL POINTS

An individual vine on an arch, tripod, or lattice becomes a focal point in a garden. Plant a beautiful vine on a simple stake. An old hoe can serve as a post for American bittersweet, and a chain link fence will support cup-and-saucer vine. Cover a decorative structure with an ordinary vine. An attractive pergola or arch becomes a

Vines, such as this nearly neon bougainvillea, can be focal points in the garden.

focal point; so do ornamental posts. For even greater drama, match the structure with a vine of a complementary color; grow yellow-leaved hops, for example, on a purple lattice, or purple-leaved sweet potato on a dwarf blue spruce.

A series of arches or tripods becomes the focal point and major element of the landscape. A series of vertical posts covered by vines forms a colonnade. Walking through it may remind you of walking through a tree-lined path or a cathedral.

BACKLIGHT

Translucent leaves modulate and modify light as it passes through, emphasizing the architecture of the plant. A wonderful effect was achieved in a New York City apartment by planting Virginia creeper in a pot on a fire escape outside a south-facing window. Every sunny day, spring through fall, the sunlight made this common, inexpensive vine look dramatic.

UNIFY YOUR GARDEN

The colors and textures of vines that cover vast expanses pull the entire landscape together. Even without flowers, the effect is striking. Dark vines, like English and Boston ivies, or climbing hydrangea, add depth and appear to extend the outer reaches of your garden, making it seem larger than it is.

Vines are great blenders in the landscape, serving as backdrops for colorful flowers. Flowering climbers become walls of color, which not only add a vertical plane to flat space, but complement the bloom of other plants. After blooming, they are quiet, reflective; against their dark and textured foliage, other flowers shine.

Vines mimic fabrics in the landscape. Allow them to hang down from above and they form curtains that ripple in even the gentlest breeze. Fine-textured vines allow dappled light through their foliage, forming a semitransparent screen that encourages the eye to look beyond.

The visual mass of large vines is strong in color and texture. A background of dark vines appears to recede.

Vines unify the garden, quietly blending and knitting together different elements.

Allow greens to offer a calming background to these elegant white blooms.

THE VINE'S THE LIMIT

Your garden can be practical. It can be functional and plain. It can also be an Eden—your world apart—and vines can set its theme.

A tropical, jungly effect is achieved with the hardy Dutchman's pipe.

Bougainvillea helps bring a Spanish flair to this entry garden in the Southwest.

Vines can take you forward into fantasy or bring back memories you adore, create the romance of a cottage garden, or be clipped and austere. They can emphasize the plantings of your region with a local flair or bring a tropical jungle to your own backyard.

Lush and rampant foliage adds a sense of age. Tangled stems seem wild and mysterious. Vines make hideouts and intriguing places to play. A large-leaved Dutchman's pipe looks tropical year-round (it's fully hardy in much of the country). Its flowers and fruits are playful, and, grown at eye-level, perfect for the young at heart.

Special design effects, such as topiary and espalier, appear more formal and highly maintained. Clingers cover sphagnum-moss-stuffed frames for quick topiary. Vines follow wires on walls to become architectural espaliers. Hang wires over an open space and the vine becomes a living swag. Turn a climber into a treelike form with a stake and lots of pruning, and remember: vines are forgiving of mistakes. If a branch is incorrectly pruned or dies, a new one is trained easily in its place. A hole in a yew topiary could take a decade to recover; damage to a climber will be repaired after one or two growing seasons.

Vines extend upward the natural bounty of your food garden. Kiwis, beans, maypops, and grapes are as useful in the general landscape as they are in the kitchen.

Vines will make your own intimate wildlife paradise. The flowers of trumpet vine, trumpet honeysuckle, and cardinal climber attract hummingbirds, and grapes, Boston ivy, and Virginia creeper attract birds in late fall.

Vines can produce food and be beautiful.

Hummingbirds feed on such vines as trumpet vine, trumpet honeysuckle, and cypress vine.

A honeysuckle lends a sense of age and wildness to a cottage garden.

Use fast-growing vines like sweet autumn clematis to create drama in a single season.

Topiaries and espaliers can be made with vines, such as English ivy, at left, and creeping fig, below. Vines have an advantage over other woody plants for such effects because they are forgiving. New shoots are easily trained to fill in holes.

Dipper gourds, such as these at Longwood Gardens, are fascinating to children. Annual gourds grow big quickly in just one summer.

COLOR WITH VINES

A hybrid clematis caps a white picket fence.

Fruit, such as those on this purple-leaved grape, extend the colorful effect of vines.

Vines can be bold, and they can be subtle. They can be showy for a moment or a season. Or they can quietly impress with shimmering shades of rich greens. Spring and summer bloomers can bring a wall of color to your garden. Their effect may be fleeting as it is with the gorgeous rambling rose—or long-lasting, as with mandevilla or golden trumpet. They can perform solo, or extend harmoniously the colors of another plant.

A Silver Moon rambler rose in a Japanese tree lilac doubles the effect of cream-colored flowers in June. Such complementary plantings enhance the beauty of both.

Don't be mistaken—showy doesn't always mean a riot of color. It can also mean quiet, understated, elegant. And it's not just flowers that put on such a show. The foliage of vines, their fruit, and winter structure all make equal statements in your landscape.

Sweet potato vine cultivars have purple or yellow foliage throughout the summer. The yellow autumn color of climbing hydrangea is followed by dry, pinkish-buff flowers and flaky cinnamon winter bark. Boston ivy and Virginia creeper have exceptionally attractive autumn red leaves. Textures abound in vines; the large leaves of Dutchman's pipe, moonflower, and kiwi contrast with the cut or small leaves of cypress vine, clematis, and climbing snapdragons.

Foliage can be showy throughout the growing season. Here, the evergreen leaves of Gold Heart English ivy add year-long color.

The bold texture of Dutchman's pipe makes a strong statement in the garden. Its texture is substantial throughout the growing season and shows up well on moonlit nights, when color fades away.

VINES WITH LONG-LASTING INTEREST

Trumpet honeysuckle (*Lonicera sempervirens*)
Climbing hydrangea (*Hydrangea*)
Moonlight schizophragma (*Schizophragma hydrangeoides*)
Trumpet vine (*Campsis radicans*)
Mandevilla (*Mandevilla*)
Golden trumpet (*Allamanda*)
Kolomikta vine (*Actinidia kolomikta*)
Bougainvillea (*Bougainvillea*)
Hybrid clematis (*Clematis*)
Hyacinth bean (*Dolichos lablab*)
Moonflower (*Ipomoea alba*)

Autumn is a time to celebrate seasonal change, and the more color the better. Vines such as Virginia creeper shown above produce a curtain of fall color.

Winter seems shorter when there are beautiful things to see. Plant a vine with attractive bark and flower stalks, such as this climbing hydrangea, and enjoy it from your window.

Plant vines on vines for twice the effect. Here, Jackman clematis entwines a rambling rose.

BLOOM AND GROW

Vines with showy flowers are a joy to use. They add luxuriant color and do not take up space. Some bloom with one brief burst of color, others blossom throughout the growing season. Trumpet honeysuckle blooms from May until October. Tropical vines such as mandevilla and golden trumpet (planted as annuals) bloom the entire summer. Three selections of clematis will give you spring-to-fall flowers: anemone clematis in spring, Jackman clematis in summer, and sweet autumn clematis in fall. With planning, flowers will span the seasons.

White, yellow, and orange shine at a distance against dark green and purple. White shows up on dark nights and is perfect near patios where you spend evenings.

When wisteria blooms, spring has arrived. The long, fragrant strands are a welcome sign after winter. Wisteria typically is purple, but white and rose selections are available. Cultivars with double flowers last a bit longer.

VINES FOR SPRING BLOOM

Anemone clematis (*Clematis montana*)
Golden clematis (*Clematis tangutica*)
Roses (*Rosa*)
Evergreen clematis (*Clematis cirrhosa* and *C. armandii*)
Wisteria (*Wisteria*)
Sweet pea (*Lathyrus odoratus*)
Carolina jessamine (*Gelsemium sempervirens*)

Annual sweet peas are old favorites that are fragrant and should be planted by seed each year, early in the spring.

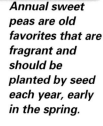

Carolina jessamine is a southern favorite noted for its early bloom.

Dark purples and blues add contrast to a bright border, and complement yellows and oranges; purple shows off against the silver of some conifers.

Bright colors are just what you need to show off flowers in a dark area.

Experiment with colors and combinations. If the flowers look appealing in a catalog, check to see if the vine will grow in your area, figure out what support it needs, and then buy it. If the color doesn't seem to work, move it or replace it. In most cases, you'll love the effect—the "accident" is what makes gardening fun.

Plant vines with other plants that have similar flowers or fruit or with structures painted to emphasize color combinations, such as lavender and yellow, purple and rose, or purple and orange. Use these combinations in the garden. Mix vines, perennials, and shrubs together. Paint structures in colors that you like and plant vines that contrast or match.

Hybrid clematis provides a sheet of color during the early part of the summer.

Sweet autumn clematis is fragrant in late summer. Its white flowers show up even at night.

It is obvious why roses are so popular on fences. Shown here, Blaze rambling rose.

VINES FOR SUMMER BLOOM

Moonflower (*Ipomoea alba*)
Jackman clematis (*Clematis × jackmanii*)
Hyacinth bean (*Dolichos lablab*)
Climbing rose (some) (*Rosa*)
Coral vine (*Antigonon leptopus*)
Cross vine (*Bignonia*)
Trumpet vine (*Campsis radicans*)
Mandevilla (*Mandevilla*)
Golden trumpet (*Allamanda*)
Bougainvillea (*Bougainvillea*)

VINES FOR FRAGRANCE

Evergreen clematis (*Clematis armandii, C. cirrhosa*)
Anemone clematis (*Clematis montana*)
Sweet autumn clematis (*Clematis terniflora*)
Moonflower (*Ipomoea alba*)
Roses (some) (*Rosa*)
Carolina jessamine (*Gelsemium sempervirens*)
Pink Chinese jasmine (*Jasminum polyanthum*)
Madagascar jasmine (*Stephanotis floribunda*)
Confederate jasmine (*Trachelospermum jasminoides*)
Wisteria (*Wisteria*)

THE ELEGANCE OF GREENS

The soothing greens of vine foliage can add substance to a garden. Star jasmine, needlepoint ivy, and creeping fig flank an arch, while wisteria climbs in the background.

VINES WITH DARK GREEN FOLIAGE

Boston ivy (*Parthenocissus tricuspidata*)
Dutchman's pipe (*Aristolochia*)
Cardinal climber (*Ipomoea quamoclit*)
Akebia (*Akebia*)
Morning glory (*Ipomoea tricolor*)
Evergreen clematis (*Clematis armandii*)

Green, of course, is the fundamental color of the garden. It's the "ground" on which the other colors show. It ties the space together through the seasons and allows the eye to rest. But look again. This single green is not so simple, after all. It's a range of shades from the light and yellow green of spring to the dark blue-green of summer growth. It's glossy and it's dull, and with the foliage of your vines, their hues and textures, you can make a quiet place—a space with an elegance all its own.

THE LAYERED LOOK

Experiment with two- and three-dimensional effects. Some vines, such as Boston ivy, are flat and tightly clinging. They create a fantastic wall of green. Contrast this with a vine that grows horizontally. Climbing hydrangea and false climbing hydrangea escape the plane by sending out horizontal shoots on which their flowers bloom. English ivy, bougainvillea, and trumpet vine also stand out from walls.

The leaves of Dutchman's pipe are bold and dark. They grow in layers and lend a tropical three-dimensional effect to the garden. The foliage of kiwi is even larger, and new growth is covered with orange hairs. Look closely for the shimmer of color.

FINE-TEXTURED GRACE

Fine-textured and translucent leaves bring lightness and grace to the garden, and counter any heaviness in the landscape. Plant kiwi between you and the sun and explore the veins of the leaves in a way you never thought possible. Use an Italian clematis as a

Golden hop has chartreuse leaves.

Compacta English ivy

screen; its sense of lacy intrigue offers glimpses of what is beyond. The 'Lowii' cultivar of Boston ivy has small leaves like many clematis. For the smallest and finest leaves of all, plant cypress vine.

GLOSSY OR MUTED?

Glossy green leaves shimmer in the sun. Some of the cultivars of English ivy glisten all year long. Wintercreeper and evergreen clematis are two other shiny evergreens; Boston ivy is deciduous. In contrast are the muted shades of Virginia creeper, akebia, and Siberian gooseberry, as well as the matte finish of schizophragma 'Moonlight'. These are much quieter in the landscape and make great backdrops.

The grapes and roses over this arbor create a dramatic kaleidoscope of greenery and light.

VINES WITH FINE TEXTURE

Climbing bleeding heart (*Dicentra scandens*)
Anemone clematis (*Clematis montana*)
Cardinal climber (*Ipomoea x multifida*)
Pink Chinese jasmine (*Jasminum polyanthum*)
Silver lace vine (*Polygonum aubertii*)
Confederate jasmine (*Trachelospermum jasminoides*)
Climbing snapdragon (*Asarina scandens*)
Italian clematis (*Clematis viticella*)
Sweet autumn clematis (*C. terniflora*)
Cypress vine (*Ipomoea quamoclit*)

VINES WITH BOLD TEXTURE

Dutchman's pipe (*Aristolochia macrophylla*)
Moonflower (*Ipomoea alba*)
Kiwi (*Actinidia deliciosa*)
Algerian ivy (*Hedera canariensis*)
Wood vamp (*Decumaria barbara*)
Trumpet vine (*Campsis radicans*)
Cup-and-saucer vine (*Cobaea scandens*)
Ornamental gourd (*Cucurbita pepo*)
Hops (*Humulus*)
Bottle gourd (*Lagenaria siceraria*)
Crimson glory vine (*Vitis coignetiae*)

A deeply lobed cultivar of English ivy, Hedera helix 'Midget', provides especially fine texture.

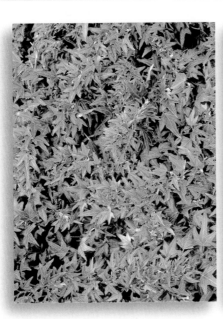

The bold leaves of crimson glory vine (Vitis coignetiae)

BOLD AND COLORFUL LEAVES

Leaf color lasts throughout the season and is more enduring in the landscape than flowers or fruit. Color choices include yellow, white, purple, and pink. Left to right: golden hops, variegated wintercreeper, and Emerald 'n Gold wintercreeper (in winter).

The foliage of vines can be as splashy and dramatic as their flowers, and since leaf color can be both a constant and a changing element in the garden, plan for it with care. Consider all the flowers that will appear through the season so you avoid unwanted combinations. Be sure you won't tire of the leaf color halfway through the summer, and remember that some leaves will change color in both the spring and fall.

RANGE OF COLORS

Foliage color offers a wide variety of choices. There are vines with leaves that are entirely purple, yellow, or chartreuse. Others have variegated leaves that are usually marked by a mix of green with white, yellow, or even pink.

Play with foliage colors. Try purple leaves with pink flowers. Mix them with petunias, roses, and other pink-flowered plants. Orange, surprisingly, is smashing with purple. Consider annual zinnias, Mexican sunflowers, and other orange flowers near purple-leaved vines. Blue foliage, especially blue conifers, goes well with purple. Plant a hyacinth bean to grow on a concolor fir, or a Blackie sweet potato vine in a container at the base of a dwarf Japanese white pine.

Yellow leaves brighten dark areas and can match the yellows of flowers grown among them. A yellow vine in front of dark brown

Buttercup English ivy has soft yellow, evergreen leaves.

Purple-leaved grape leaves deepen to rich dark purple in autumn.

YELLOWS
Buttercup English ivy (*Hedera helix*)
Gold Leaf Algerian ivy (*Hedera colchica*)
Margarita sweet potato (*Ipomoea batatas*)
Golden hops (*Humulus*)

PURPLES
Purple sweet potato (*Ipomoea batatas* 'Blackie')
Purpleleafed wintercreeper (*Euonymus fortunei*)
Hyacinth bean (*Dolichos lablab*)
Purpleleafed grape (*Vitis vinifera* 'Purpurea')

timbers is a knockout. The chartreuse of the Margarita sweet potato vine will brighten a dark container of evergreens. And if you have a bed of black-eyed susans, try a bamboo tripod with black-eyed susan vine nearby to give some height and to repeat the gold and brown.

COMPLEMENTARY STRUCTURES

Paint trellises, pots, arbors, and other structures a color complementary to the vine. For example, paint a trellis yellow and plant it with a purple-leaved grape. Purple-leaved sweet potato is easy in a pot. Trail it out of a concrete container that has been painted orange or pink. Try yellow-leaved ivy on dark brick, or variegated hops on a dark evergreen.

VARIEGATED LEAVES
Variegated Japanese hops (*Humulus japonicus*)
Kolomikta vine (*Actinidia kolomikta*)
Wintercreeper (*Euonymus*)
Variegated akebia (*Akebia quinata*)

Fall color is the final burst of life before the quiet of winter. Vines complement the autumn color of trees. Shown here, climbing hydrangea.

AUTUMN COLOR

Autumn color is one of the joys of living in a climate with four distinct seasons. We usually think of trees when we think of fall color, but there are vines that are equally vibrant. They let you mix and match. Grow a vine with yellow fall foliage (climbing hydrangea) on the trunk of a tree with red fall color (pin oak, sour gum, sweet gum) for a trunk of yellow and a blaze of red or purple in the crown. Reverse the effect with the red of Boston ivy or Virginia creeper on a tulip tree.

Three vines for excellent fall color (top to bottom): Boston ivy, Virginia creeper, crimson glory vine.

The crisp white and green leaves of Glacier English ivy

AUTUMN COLOR
Boston ivy (*Parthenocissus tricuspidata*)
Virginia creeper (*Parthenocissus quinquefolia*)
Climbing hydrangea (*Hydrangea petiolaris*)
Crimson glory vine (*Vitis coignetiae*)

Kolomikta vine produces tri-colored leaves that are green, white, and pink.

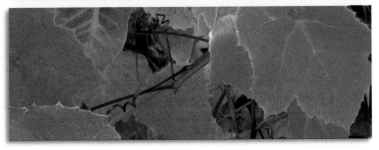

THE LATE SHOW

American bittersweet is one of the prettiest fruits of autumn. This endangered plant should not be picked in the wild. Nurseries sell it, and when planted in your own garden, you can enjoy the berries on the vine or in cut arrangements. Its Asian cousin is a noxious weed throughout the eastern United States.

Seed heads on a golden clematis

Virginia creeper's blue fruit ripen among its autumn leaves.

VINES WITH SHOWY FRUIT

American bittersweet
(*Celastrus scandens*)
Virginia creeper
(*Parthenocissus quinquefolia*)
Sweet autumn clematis
(*Clematis terniflora*)
Trumpet honeysuckle
(*Lonicera sempervirens*)
Hyacinth bean
(*Dolichos lablab*)
Ornamental gourd
(*Cucurbita pepo*)
Pepper vine
(*Ampelopsis arborea*)

A fascinating garden is more than just flowers and foliage. And at the end of the growing season, when other colors pale—even autumn leaves—vines can be dramatic. They bring an upward moving brightness to the fall and winter.

SHOWY FRUITS

Probably the most famous vine for fruit is American bittersweet. It, or more often its weedy Asian cousin, is picked for autumn arrangements. Unfortunately, American bittersweet has become a rare plant in the wild. Growing it in your garden is one way to help increase its numbers. You'll need both a male and female plant for fruit to set.

Not everyone realizes that gourds and squash grow on vines. These showy fruits add interest to both the ornamental and the vegetable garden. Train them—and pumpkins—on arbors or small trees; let the fruit hang down. There is nothing quite like walking under a pumpkin! But be sure to choose one of the smaller-fruited selections.

Porcelain vines have extremely showy fruit. They look like miniature pieces of porcelain, varying in color from speckled white to violet to blue. Unfortunately, birds love them and spread this Asian plant into natural areas. In some parts of the country—especially the Northeast—it becomes an invasive weed. Try its American cousin, pepper vine, for more quietly beautiful berries.

Virginia creeper bears fruit that look like miniature Concord grapes. They are attractive, but what really sets them off are their red stalks. They won't cause you to slow down if you are driving by, but they are intriguing whenever you're close enough to walk near them.

Other fruits show off their form in interesting ways. Clematis seed heads resemble feathered headdresses, starting in the fall, then staying for early winter. Climbing hydrangea holds its old flowers and fruits through the winter, resembling dried floral arrangements.

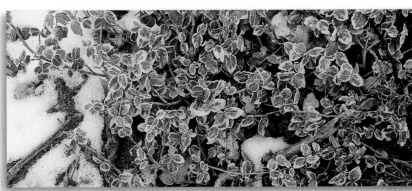

The trunks and faded flowers of climbing hydrangea are amazingly picturesque in the winter.

The evergreen effect of wintercreeper (above) and variegated Persian ivy (at left)

WINTER SILHOUETTES

Winter is a wonderful time to appreciate the "bones" of vines. The bark of climbing hydrangea "sheds" to reveal papery reddish-brown layers that become more beautiful as the plant ages. The bark of grapes peels off in distinctive long strips; an aged grape vine is a sight to behold. Old wisteria trunks twine around themselves in amazingly beautiful patterns, especially when outlined in snow. Boston ivy forms a flat, fine-textured tracery upon surfaces, especially in contrast to a yellow or ochre-colored masonry wall.

EVERGREENS

The presence of evergreens can help you get through the winter. Wintercreeper is one of the hardiest of the evergreen vines. Its cultivar 'Vegetus' climbs well and can eventually reach the top of a three-story building.

Some English ivy cultivars, such as 'Bulgaria' and 'Baltica', are nearly as hardy as euonymus. In far northern areas where they are borderline hardy, plant them along a sheltered wall and protect them from the winter sun. Some cultivars have yellow leaves; others have shapes that are distinctly different. Algerian ivy offers bolder leaves than English ivy, although it is not hardy north of zone 8.

Overwintering birds seek the shelter of evergreens. A tree trunk covered by English ivy will be alive with winter bird sounds.

In warm climates, evergreen clematis and creeping fig are good selections for evergreen vines. The clematises have shiny leaves and very showy, fragrant flowers. Creeping fig has small leaves and makes a fine-textured wall covering.

VINES FOR WINTER EFFECT

Climbing hydrangea (*Hydrangea petiolaris*)
Grape (*Vitis*)
Wisteria (*Wisteria*)
Siberian gooseberry (*Actinidia arguta*)
False climbing hydrangea (*Schizophragma hydrangeoides*)
Trumpet vine (*Campsis radicans*)

EVERGREEN VINES

Wintercreeper (*Euonymus fortunei*)
English ivy (*Hedera helix*)
Algerian ivy (*Hedera canariensis*)
Creeping fig (*Ficus pumila*)
Evergreen clematis (*Clematis cirrhosa, Clematis armandii*)
Cross vine (*Bignonia capreolata*)
Carolina jessamine (*Gelsemium sempervirens*)

COLORFUL COMPANIONS

Climbing hydrangea covers a tree trunk with flowers.

Ville de Lyon clematis seems to float amidst pine branches.

Most plants flower for only a short period each year, but you can extend their color by combining them with vines. The vines may flower in another season or at the same time to complement the color of the base plant. Vines also bring color to plants that do not have showy flowers or fruit, such as evergreens.

Worried that the vine will kill its supporting plant? Selection is the key. Don't plant a vine that will overwhelm or outgrow its partner. If the plant is small, do not plant a vigorous vine with heavy stems and foliage. And keep this in mind: You can always cut a vine at its base to control its vigor and growth. If you want to remove it, paint its stump with an herbicide.

VINES ON TREE TRUNKS

Plant a flowering vine at the base of a large tree, and in a few years the trunk will appear to bloom. Choose vines that tolerate shade, do not twine, and bloom to complement or contrast. Rootlet vines are easiest to use because they cling without any help. Plant small vines to minimize disturbance to the roots of the tree. Extra water and fertilizer the first year will get it started. Try climbing hydrangea, false climbing hydrangea, and wood vamp. All bloom well in the shade and hold their flowers away from the trunk.

Tendril-type vines will not climb tree trunks by themselves. Cover part of the trunk with netting to help them. Or plant a tendril vine on a rootlet vine. For instance, plant English ivy at the base of a tree. After it is established, plant a clematis. The clematis will cling by itself to the ivy, and you will have flowers in summer from the clematis and evergreen leaves from the ivy all year.

English ivy makes a beautiful evergreen covering. But ivy is vigorous enough to eventually overwhelm and shade out even large trees. If you find the ivy is within the top 20 to 30 feet of a tree, consider cutting it at the base and letting it climb again.

COVERING BARE LEGS

Some plants are bare at their base, and you may feel they need some dressing up. Vines are the perfect cover. Plant a flowering vine, such as hybrid clematis or purple bell vine, at the base of a viburnum. You will hide the bare stems and have blooms during the summer.

Likewise, shrubs or perennials can cover the bare base of some vines. It will look as if the rose or clematis is coming up through the middle of the other plants, and its bare base will be totally hidden.

VINES ON OTHER PLANTS

You can combine vines with small trees, shrubs, even perennials. Try a blooming vine on a pine tree. You will surprise your friends when they notice you have a pine with blossoms. Many gardeners have had good luck training rambling roses onto old apple trees. The apples bloom in the spring, followed by the roses in early summer.

Tree peonies bloom in the spring and then are green the rest of the summer. Plant a hybrid clematis to grow on the peony. You'll have summer flowers, yet the clematis will not shade out the peony. Sweet autumn clematis and anemone clematis are both too vigorous for a small shrub. Either could, however, be trained on a mature Japanese maple and, with annual pruning, would not overwhelm it.

COMPLEMENTARY COMBINATIONS

Consider color when you combine vines with other plants. Plant purple-flowered Jackman clematis on purple-fruited beautyberry. The clematis blooms in the summer and beautyberry colors in autumn.

The Jackman clematis and beautyberry combo is good for other reasons, too. The beautyberry needs to show off in its one season: autumn. Jackman clematis and other hybrid clematis that flower on new wood can be pruned back in late summer if they've gotten too big. They'll grow enough the next spring to produce blossoms in the summer. Anemone clematis, in contrast, is vigorous and blooms on old wood; if cut back in late summer, it will not bloom the following spring. So consider complementary growth habits when combining vines.

Nelly Moser clematis on white Japanese wisteria

Golden Hop on a Colorado Blue Spruce

Niobe clematis with Mme. Louis Leveque rose

Heavenly Blue morning glory with sunflowers

Virginia creeper and variegated Persian ivy

Golden clematis and glory flower (Eccremocarpus)

SUGGESTED COMBINATIONS

Coral vine on crape myrtle
Silver Moon rose on Japanese tree lilac
Jackman clematis on beautyberry
Climbing or rambling rose on crabapple

VINES TO GROW ON TREES

Climbing hydrangea (*Hydrangea petiolans*)
False climbing hydrangea (*Schizophragma hydrangeoides*)
Wood vamp (*Decumaria*)
Anemone clematis (*Clematis montana* var. *rubens*)
Rambling roses (*Rosa*)
Trumpet vine (*Campsis*)
Carolina jessamine (*Gelsemium*)
Cross vine (*Bignonia*)
Wintercreeper (*Euonymus fortunei*)

VINES TO GROW ON SMALL PLANTS

Hybrid clematis (*Clematis*)
Durand clematis (*Clematis × durandii*)
Climbing snapdragon (*Asarina*)
Annual sweet pea (*Lathyrus odoratus*)
Purple bell vine (*Rhodochiton atrosanguineus*)
Potato vine (*Solanum jasminoides*)
Nasturtium (*Tropaeolum majus*)

PERFECT VINE, PERFECT PLACE

Cold winters can affect your choice of vines. In zones 7 and colder, most subtropical vines won't survive outdoors over winter. The more northern regions tend to have short, cool summers. The more southern areas often have long, hot summers. Above: climbing hydrangea in summer and winter.

VINES FOR COLD CLIMATES

Climbing hydrangea *(Hydrangea)*
Virginia creeper *(Parthenocissus)*
Boston ivy *(Parthenocissus)*
Siberian gooseberry *(Actinidia)*
Hops *(Humulus)*
Trumpet honeysuckle *(Lonicera)*
Dutchman's pipe *(Aristolochia)*
Trumpet vine *(Campsis)*
Silver lace vine *(Polygonum)*
American bittersweet *(Celastrus)*
Wintercreeper *(Euonymus)*
Kentucky wisteria *(Wisteria)*
Large-flowered hybrid clematis *(Clematis)*

If successful gardening could be reduced to a single rule it would be this: Select the right plant for the conditions in which it will grow. Follow that rule with vines and you'll save time, money, and frustration, and virtually guarantee success. In general, vines are quite adaptable to climatic and soil conditions, so first do a little research on your climate and the conditions in your garden. It can go a long way in helping you match your choices with local temperature ranges, rainfall, light, and soil conditions.

TEMPERATURE AND HARDINESS ZONES

The United States Department of Agriculture (USDA) has divided the U.S. and Canada into eleven hardiness zones based on average annual minimum winter temperatures. Zone 1 is the coldest and zone 11 the warmest. The map is reproduced on page 92. Knowing the zone for your area will help you determine which vines will likely survive in your garden.

For instance, if a plant is listed as being hardy to zone 4, that means that zone 4 is the coldest zone in which it will survive. If you live in zone 8, which is much warmer, the same plant will have no trouble with the winter low temperatures. It may or may not have problems with summer heat. Conversely, if you live in zone 4 and want to plant a vine that's hardy to zone 8, it may do well during the summer, but if left outside during the winter, it will die.

LIGHT

After determining if a vine is hardy for your area, consider its light requirements. "Full sun" means the location is sunny from early morning until sunset, with no shade from trees or structures. "Partial shade" locations receive direct sun for about half the day (the east side of a building, for instance) or are affected by light shade from tall trees. "Heavy or full shade" means the location never receives direct sunlight, perhaps because of trees or a structure.

VINES FOR AREAS WITH MILD WINTERS

Coral vine (*Antigonon*)
Evergreen clematis (*Clematis cirrhosa*,
   C. armandii)
Ivies (*Hedera*)
Jessamine (*Gelsemium*)
Cross vine (*Bignonia*)
Maypop (*Passiflora*)
Wood vamp (*Decumaria*)
False climbing hydrangea (*Schizophragma*)
Wisteria (*Wisteria*)
Grape (*Vitis*)
Rose (*Rosa*)
Climbing bleeding heart (*Dicentra*)
Trumpet vine (*Campsis*)
Confederate jasmine (*Trachelospermum*)

Cold temperatures are not a major concern in areas of mild winters (zones 8 and warmer). Plants in these zones face summer heat and humidity in the Southeast, drought and heat in the Southwest, and lack of heat and light and the seasonal rainfall in the Pacific Northwest. Choose vines that will do well in your climate.

Full-sun vines planted in the shade will have little vigor and rarely bloom. Full-shade vines planted in the sun will suffer from water stress which may turn the leaves brown, and can kill the plant.

SOILS

Plants require water during the growing season. If you garden in a desert area, plant vines suitable for drought or water them regularly. If your soil does not drain readily, plant cross vine, trumpet vine, bittersweet, and wood vamp; they tolerate wet soils.

Garden soils can exhibit a wide range of fertility and pH (a measure of acidity or alkalinity). Although many vines are adaptable to soil conditions that would be unfavorable to other plants, it would be well to have your soil tested for fertility, pH, and drainage properties. Contact your local extension office. They (and many private laboratories) conduct such tests, and the results can include recommendations for soil improvements. A pH of 7 is neutral. A slightly acidic rating of 6.5 is ideal for most garden plants. Unless you live in areas of high pH (alkaline soils) or low pH (acidic soils), vines will tolerate your soil. Coral vine, actinidias, porcelain vine, Dutchman's pipe, cross vine, trumpet vine, ivies, hydrangea, polygonum, grapes, and wisterias tolerate alkaline soils. Honeysuckle can tolerate very acid soils.

Mediterranean climates are noted for their mild, wet winters and dry, hot, sunny summers. Southern parts of the Pacific coast have a Mediterranean climate. Many plants have trouble surviving the long, dry summers. Summer irrigation can overcome seasonal droughts and greatly expand the number of usable plants.

VINES FOR MEDITERRANEAN CLIMATES

Bougainvillea (*Bougainvillea*)
Potato vine (*Solanum*)
Rose (*Rosa*)
Grape (*Vitis*)
Wisteria (*Wisteria*)
Glory flower (*Eccremocarpus*)
Passionflower (*Passiflora*)
Creeping fig (*Ficus*)
Ivy (*Hedera*)

South walls tend to be warm, dry locations and are just the place to experiment with vines that are not quite hardy for your region. Here, a rambler rose, 'Tausendschon', is trained up a wall in full sun.

VINES FOR HOT SUN

Trumpet vine (*Campsis*)
Virginia creeper
   (*Parthenocissus*)
English ivy (*Hedera*)
Rose (*Rosa*)
Coral vine (*Antigonon*)
Kiwi (*Actinidia*)
Siberian gooseberry
   (*Actinidia*)
Grape (*Vitis*)
Bougainvillea
   (*Bougainvillea*)
Mandevilla (*Mandevilla*)
Golden trumpet
   (*Allamanda*)
Sweet potato vine
   (*Ipomoea*)

North walls are cooler and moister locations. Here English ivy helps create seclusion.

VINES FOR SHADE

Kolomikta vine
   (*Actinidia*)
Akebia (*Akebia*)
Dutchman's pipe
   (*Aristolochia*)
Climbing hydrangea
   (*Hydrangea*)
False climbing
   hydrangea
   (*Schizophragma*)
Wood vamp
   (*Decumaria*)
Honeysuckle
   (*Lonicera*)
Creeping fig (*Ficus*)

Use vines to escape or avoid dry shade. Plant a shade-tolerant vine such as English ivy just outside the overhang of a roof and train it to grow toward the building.

VINES FOR DROUGHT

Wisteria (*Wisteria*)
Bougainvillea
   (*Bougainvillea*)
English ivy (*Hedera*)
Coral vine (*Antigonon*)
Cross vine (*Bignonia*)
Trumpet vine
   (*Campsis*)
Bittersweet (*Celastrus*)
Maypop (*Passiflora*)
Silver lace vine
   (*Polygonum*)

KNOW YOUR MICROCLIMATES

To learn what will grow well in your area, take an inventory of the microclimates in your landscape. These are individual (sometimes small) areas of your garden in which light, temperature, wind, and moisture rates will vary (sometimes considerably) from one another.

LIGHT AND TEMPERATURE

Light is easy to understand. The north side of a house is shady; the south and west sides, sunny. The north side tends to be cooler and does not dry out as quickly. The closer a garden area is to the house, the shadier and drier it is. The south and west sides are warmer, drier, and may be half a zone warmer in winter. If you want to take the risk of growing a vine that is not fully hardy in your area, try the west or south side of the house, especially if it is protected from wind.

WIND

Wind is both a blessing and a curse. Too much wind dries plants and soils quickly, but a lack of wind can facilitate fungal diseases. Notice which areas of your garden are regularly hit by winds and either establish windbreaks or use plants that are wind and drought tolerant. A few vines, including wood vamp, Dutchman's pipe, creeping fig, and false climbing hydrangea, do not tolerate strong winds well and survive best in sheltered sites. Coral vine, scarlet clematis, and golden clematis tolerate strong winds.

Wind near major highways and the ocean may carry salt, which dries out leaves and soil. Few vines tolerate salt, but coral vine, cross vine, sweet autumn clematis, Carolina jessamine, ivies, jasmine, and most roses will tolerate some salt.

MOISTURE

Rainfall varies within a region, and the moisture content of the soil can vary within a garden. Low areas tend to be wet and may never dry out. High, rocky locations are dry.

The combination of drought and shade is one of the toughest challenges for a gardener. Roof overhangs and tree roots are two of the most common causes of dry shade. Plant shade-tolerant vines just outside the overhang or at the outside of the tree roots. These sites receive a bit more moisture. Then encourage the vine to grow toward the dry shade.

VINES IN CONTAINERS: WHAT TO GROW

Containers can be microclimates of their own, and vines in containers require different care than plants in the ground. They'll need more water and fertilizer. Drought-tolerant vines are best for containers, since water stress is a common problem. Water permanent containers even during the winter months whenever the soil is dry and not frozen.

SPACE: Containers restrict root space. Large containers offset this, but a small increase in size becomes significantly heavier. Large containers are likely to need a permanent location. Grow small vines in small containers on decks, balconies, and roofs; large containers may be too heavy.

Above-ground space may be limited in small, urban gardens and on balconies and rooftops. Generally, vines that are not overly vigorous have the best chance of surviving restricted space.

HARDINESS: Containers left outside year-round have their own hardiness challenges. The roots of plants in above-ground containers are exposed to lower temperatures than plants in the ground. A plant rated for zone 6 will survive in the ground in that zone, but it may suffer winter injury in a container. The smaller and less insulated the container, the more severe this problem.

There are no hard-and-fast rules for the hardiness of plant roots. Select vines that are rated as hardy one or two zones colder than your climate. These are most likely to be root hardy. If you buy small and inexpensive vines for your trials, you won't lose much if they die.

Many English ivy selections are good for year-round container plantings in zones 7 and warmer. They are also drought tolerant and grow in sun or shade.

Some tropical vines, like this Red Riding Hood mandevilla that blooms all summer, are easily grown as annuals.

CONTAINER VINES IN THE NORTH: TENDER OR HARDY?

Northerners can enjoy tropical vines in containers. Most bloom all summer and have attractive foliage. Most are inexpensive enough to replace each year. They can be brought inside for the winter, into a greenhouse, or in front of a sunny window, or kept dormant in a cool, dark area at about 40° F. Any of the annual vines are perfect for containers.

A hardy vine in a container provides versatility. Use it in a prominent spot while it blooms. Then move it into sun to build up strength for next year's flowers. Shown here: Clematis florida sieboldii.

HARDY VINES
Virginia creeper (*Parthenocissus*)
Boston ivy (*Parthenocissus*)
Climbing hydrangea (*Hydrangea*)
False climbing hydrangea (*Schizophragma*)
Kentucky wisteria (*Wisteria*)
Yellow honeysuckle (*Lonicera*)
Hops (*Humulus*)
Dutchman's pipe (*Aristolochia*)
Trumpet vine (*Campsis*)
Silver lace vine (*Polygonum*)
American bittersweet (*Celastrus*)
Large-flowered hybrid clematis (*Clematis*)

TENDER VINES
Mandevilla (*Mandevilla*)
Golden trumpet (*Allamanda*)
Sweet potato vine (*Ipomoea*)
Potato vine (*Solanum*)
Bougainvillea (*Bougainvillea*)
Blue pea (*Clitoria*)
Glory flower (*Eccremocarpus*)
Passion flower (*Passiflora*)
Purple bell vine (*Rhodochiton*)

HOW VINES GROW

When you select a structure, it is essential that you know how a vine grows, its vigor, size, and weight, so you can select the right support. Vines grow in four different ways—twining, clinging by rootlets, clinging by tendrils, and climbing/sprawling. These growth habits are illustrated below, and each vine has its own ideal type of support. Trying to make a vine climb a structure not suited to it will only result in frustration. Vigorous vines need large, strong structures to support their mass. Petite vines can grow on light structures.

A morning glory on a post

Wisteria on a strong arbor

TWINERS

Hyacinth bean on chain link

Hops on lattice

Twiners wrap their stems around a vertical object. They grow on posts, chain-link fences, arbors, and lattices. Do not grow them on living trees because they can strangle and kill the tree.

CLINGING ROOTLETS

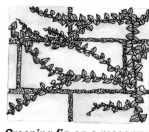

Creeping fig on a masonry wall

Wintercreeper covering a rock pile

Climbing hydrangea on a tree trunk

These plants have rootlets (some have adhesive discs) along the stem that attach to their support, such as a masonry wall, tree trunk, or rock pile. Some will grow on banks as a ground cover. They are not parasites and draw no nourishment from their support structure.

NOT TO WORRY

Do you remember how Sleeping Beauty's castle became covered and entwined with vines? Many people do. They worry about vines damaging structures and getting out of hand.

Selection is the key; it will bring joy rather than misery to your garden. By knowing how each vine grows, as well as how quickly, you can choose a vine that will be an asset rather than a problem.

Avoid damage to buildings by keeping rootlet-type vines away from wood structures and by making sure any masonry to be covered is in good condition. Do not use vines like wallpaper, to cover problems instead of fixing them. Be cautious in the use of vigorous climbers and choose ones whose ultimate size matches the structure on which they are growing.

Vigorous vines are useful in certain situations. Vigor, for instance, is a virtue when you have a four-story masonry wall to cover. Trumpet vine, Virginia creeper, and English ivy can be valuable in such a case. In most other cases, a less vigorous vine will need less maintenance.

TENDRILS

Tendrils essentially reach out to attach to something. Tendrils are actually modified stems, but some vines (such as clematis) have modified leaves that also act as tendrils. Tendril vines cling well to shrubs, chain link, strings, netting, and thin lattice. A few vines have tendrils with adhesive tips. Some of these plants combine the qualities of tendril and rootlet vines.

Passionflower tendrils clinging to chain link

Clematis on a shrub

Sweet pea climbing on netting

Clematis wrapping its leaf stalks around thin lattice

CLIMBERS, SPRAWLERS

These have lax stems that sprawl over other plants and can be tied to supporting structures. Even though they are often called climbers, they have no mechanism for climbing by themselves. Climbing and rambling roses are the best-known examples, and usually need to be tied to their support.

A climbing rose tied onto lattice

A masonry anchor supports a climbing rose

Rose stems woven into a lattice

FIND GOOD SUPPORT

One of the easiest ways to use vines is to plant them on existing supports. Find the structure, think about vines that can grow on it, then choose one that will have the ornamental features you want. Vines grow on almost anything: masonry walls, trees, shrubs, fences, railings, and posts.

VINES FOR A BRICK OR STONE WALL (ROOTLET VINES)

Cross vine (*Bignonia capreolata*)
Silvervein creeper (*Parthenocissus henryana*)
Wintercreeper (*Euonymus fortunei*)
Wood vamp (*Decumaria barbara*)
Climbing hydrangea (*Hydrangea petiolaris*)
False climbing hydrangea (*Schizophragma hydrangeoides*)

Variegated wintercreeper

VINES FOR CHAIN LINK AND WROUGHT IRON (TWINERS, TENDRIL VINES)

Morning glory (*annual Ipomoea*)
Kentucky wisteria (*Wisteria macrostachya*)
Ivy (*Hedera helix*)
Moonseed (*Menispermum*)
Silver lace vine (*Polygonum*)
Confederate jasmine (*Trachelospermum jasminoides*)

Morning glory

VINES FOR AN OPEN WOOD FENCE (TWINERS)

Kolomikta vine (*Actinidia kolomikta*)
Dutchman's pipe (*Aristolochia macrophylla*)
American bittersweet (*Celastrus scandens*)
Carolina jessamine (*Gelsemium sempervirens*)

Trumpet honeysuckle

VINES ON WALLS

Are vines a threat to walls? There are two sides to this question. Most masons and carpenters advise against growing vines on masonry or wood. Most gardeners say vines are okay on masonry and stone, as long as the material is in good condition. Each group has a preference. One thing is certain: Wood is especially susceptible to damage from moisture and should not have vines rooting into it.

Vines, especially those that root into their support, hold in moisture behind their leaves and hide defects, both of which speed the decline of a wood structure.

Stucco is also likely to be damaged by rootlet vines. But gardeners report no

VINES FOR POSTS (TWINERS)

Dutchman's pipe (*Aristolochia*)
American bittersweet (*Celastrus scandens*)
Carolina jessamine (*Gelsemium sempervirens*)
Large-flowered hybrid clematis (*Clematis*)
Hops (*Humulus*)
Trumpet honeysuckle (*Lonicera sempervirens*)
Rose (if tied) (*Rosa*)
American wisteria (*Wisteria frutescens*)
Kolomikta vine (*Actinidia kolomikta*)

Niobe clematis

VINES FOR TREE STUMPS OR ROCK PILES (ROOTLET VINES)

Virginia creeper (*Parthenocissus quinquefolia*)
Trumpet vine (*Campsis radicans*)
Wood vamp (*Decumaria barbara*)
Creeping fig (*Ficus pumila*)
Ivies (*Hedera*)
Climbing hydrangea (*Hydrangea petiolaris*)
False climbing hydrangea (*Schizophragma hydrangeoides*)

Kewensis Wintercreeper

problems with them on concrete block, brick, or stone walls, as long as the masonry is in good shape at the time of planting.

Climbing hydrangea, wood vamp, and false climbing hydrangea are some of the prettiest vines for these. All bloom in late spring or early summer and have showy, creamy white flowers. Boston ivy and Virginia creeper are very vigorous vines that will quickly cover walls and provide great fall color. English ivy, similar in its vigor, is evergreen, and has a range of leaf colors and sizes. Wintercreeper is a good evergreen for the north; creeping fig works well in warm regions.

Many masonry houses have the top story sided with wood or aluminum. Do not let the vines climb over or under the siding. If your entire house has aluminum or vinyl siding, most vines will not climb on it. If you want a vine anyway, consider hanging wire netting about six inches out from the wall on which to grow vines but make sure that none of the vine works its way under the siding.

VINES ON TREES

There are two major concerns in growing a climbing vine on a living tree. The vine may strangle the tree or it may overtake it and shade it out. Generally, a large twiner, such as wisteria, will be a strangler and should not be planted on a living tree.

Rootlet climbers, such as hydrangea and wintercreeper, are excellent for a tree trunk because they are less likely to encircle it. If they do, however, cut them below the point at which the encircling begins to avoid future problems. The vines will grow straight up from the cut, and the tree will survive.

To kill the vine, cut it near the ground and paint the wound with an herbicide. A local garden center or nursery can advise which herbicide to use.

Make the cuts and apply herbicide during the growing season. Another method that reduces the untidy appearance of dying leaves is to cut down the vine in winter when it is dormant, and apply herbicide to newly emerging leaves around the stump in spring. If the vine is an evergreen, such as English ivy, winter is the best time to cut it. The leaves will gradually turn brown and look like part of the winter landscape.

Climbing hydrangea (shown here in fall color) is an excellent vine to grow up the trunks of mature trees, such as oaks.

VINES FOR ARBORS (TWINERS)

Coral vine (*Antigonon*)
Pink anemone clematis (*Clematis montana* var. *rubens*)
Large-flowered hybrid clematis (*Clematis*)
Dutchman's pipe (*Aristolochia*)
Silver lace vine (*Polygonum aubertii*)
Gourds (*Cucurbita*)
Kentucky wisteria (*Wisteria*)

Henryi Clematis

VINES FOR LATTICE (TENDRIL, SPRAWLERS, AND NON-VIGOROUS TWINING VINES)

Hybrid clematis (*Clematis*)
Rose (*Rosa*)
Kolomikta vine (*Actinidia kolomikta*)
Mandevilla (annual) (*Mandevilla*)
Golden trumpet (annual) (*Allamanda*)
Coral vine (*Antigonon*)

Mandevilla

VINES THAT NEED STRONG SUPPORTS

Some vines are extremely vigorous and need strong supports. Wisteria, akebia, trumpet creepers and even English ivy can become so strong and heavy that they destroy the structure. The Japanese and Chinese wisteria are the most likely to do this and should be planted on exceptionally strong structures. Regular pruning will control the growth of such vigorous vines and avoid damage.

WINNERS AND CHALLENGERS

So many vines, so little time. With such a multitude of colorful, hardy, and energetic vines out there, you may find yourself overwhelmed in selecting the appropriate plant. To get you started, here are our suggestions for six "winning" vines—and six you'll most likely want to "weed out" of your garden scheme.

SIX EASY VINES

Successful vines grow well in a wide range of soils and conditions, are healthy and beautiful, and do not cause additional problems. They are pest resistant and need little pruning, fertilization, and watering. They do not invade surrounding gardens or natural areas and are neat, non-toxic, and fully hardy. Most of the vines in the Selection Guide are "good guys," but the vines on this page are usually the most trouble free.

In selecting "good guy" vines, first consider varieties that are hardy in your region. Look for vines that have a moderate growth rate and don't require much care.

Find those that require the growing conditions you can provide without too much trouble, and make sure they will fit the space and structure you have for them.

Pest resistance is important, too, but keep in mind that some pests are regional. Your extension agent can advise you about pests that are a problem in your area.

Hybrid clematis 'Ville de Lyon'
(Clematis hybrids) *This is one of many cultivars in a showy group of vines that are hardy, virtually pest-free, and so lightweight you can let them scamper over perennials.*

American bittersweet
(Celastrus scandens) *Producing a stunning show of orange and red fruit in the autumn, this endangered native is untroubled by pests, quite hardy, and grows in sun or shade.*

Dutchman's pipe
(Aristolochia macrophylla) *Valued for its huge, bold leaves and fascinating flowers, this tough vine is untouched by pests. It grows in sun or shade, in the North and in the South.*

Climbing hydrangea
(Hydrangea petiolaris) *This easy-to-grow, hardy, deciduous vine offers great blooms in late spring. It is beautiful in winter with tan, dried flowers and exfoliating bark.*

Hyacinth bean
(Dolichos lablab) *This is an easy annual vine with great color appeal and a restrained habit. Full sun and good drainage are all that it needs.*

Mandevilla
(Mandevilla × amabilis) *A tropical vine easy to grow as an annual anywhere summers are warm, mandevilla requires only full sun, moderate moisture, and fertile soil.*

SIX CHALLENGING VINES

A plant can be a problem if it does things we don't want or if it causes us to spend unexpected time and effort taking care of it, even though it might be the most beautiful plant in the world. Vines are no different, and the problems you'll have are most likely to be with those that are overly vigorous or those whose growth is invasive.

Boston and English ivies, for example, can be assets in your garden, but are vigorous and need regular pruning to keep them from covering your windows or growing under shingles. Sweet autumn clematis is too vigorous to grow on other plants.

Some vines rank among the worst of weeds, and no one in their right mind would consider planting them. Poison ivy, for example, is a weedy native plant responsible for much misery over the eastern United States (for suggestions on control, please see page 51). Kudzu, Japanese honeysuckle (see page 75), and Oriental bittersweet (see page 57) are examples of vines brought to this country deliberately, albeit ignorantly, and which have since become disastrous weeds. Their invasiveness outweighs any decorative benefits they might otherwise provide, and they should never be planted in gardens.

Some vines spread invasively because birds and other wildlife carry their seeds. Others spread by root suckers and horizontal shoots. The multiflora rose, also known as the weedy rose, seeds into both gardens and natural areas and becomes a weed. It has been used as a conservation plant by some states and has become a particular nuisance in the East.

The "challengers" on this page are actually beloved in the garden, but gardeners need to understand the potential problems they can pose. Remember: plant with forethought.

Japanese wisteria
(Wisteria floribunda) *Only the hardiest of structures can withstand the weight and activity of Japanese wisteria. Choose wrought-iron or large arbors. In southern woods and wetlands it can become a weed.*

Morning glory
(Ipomoea tricolor) *One of the more high-achieving vines, morning glory can grow 10 feet per season. But because it can self-seed, it often becomes a very weedy vine, especially in the South.*

Porcelain vine
(Ampelopsis brevipedunculata) *The beautifully colored fruit of this plant attracts birds that eat and spread the seeds around. The vine can become a nasty weed in the garden and in natural areas, especially in the East.*

Five-leaved akebia
(Akebia quinata) *This innocent-looking vine invades nearby garden areas by means of horizontal shoots. These shoots root into the soil and are difficult to eradicate.*

Trumpet vine or trumpet creeper
(Campsis radicans) *Gardeners and hummingbirds alike appreciate the large, orange flowers of this vine. But watch out: it suckers and seeds aggressively.*

English ivy
(Hedera helix) *This clinging vine climbs trees with ease, and is popular for dense evergreen cover. It can require constant control to keep its rapid growth in bounds.*

GROW GREAT VINES

BUYING NEW PLANTS

Vines, like all other garden plants, are available from garden centers and mail-order outlets. Each source has its own advantages.

In a garden center you can ask questions in person. Such face-to-face information is, of course, not available from mail-order outlets, but they usually will have a greater selection.

Whether you buy from a nursery, garden center, public garden sale, plant society, or mail-order house, the most important thing is to buy quality plants from a reputable dealer.

Some vines are sold as bare-root plants; the majority, however, are container grown.

Avoid pot-bound plants whose roots totally fill and circle around the pot. Inspect the plant before buying by knocking it out of the pot (ask the nursery or garden center to do it for you).

Bare-root plants are often less expensive, and you can inspect the health of the roots directly. They should be white or tan, firm, and show a minimum of breakage.

Bare-root vines can be less expensive because they weigh less, and that reduces shipping costs. They will, however, need more immediate attention than container vines.

In either case, inspect newly purchased plants thoroughly. The roots should be firm, strong, and healthy, with a rich white or tan color, and should show little or no breakage.

Leaf and stem condition is less important (even insignificant if the vine is herbaceous and dormant), but there should be few leaves with brown edges (indicating stress) or signs of insect damage. Container-grown plants should not be pot-bound. Knock the plant out of the pot to check the roots or have the garden center staff do it for you. You can also gently dig your fingers into the top of the soil. If it seems totally filled with roots, it is probably pot-bound.

If you've purchased bare-root vines, plant them immediately, if possible. If you need to, store them cool and moist—but don't soak them; they'll rot.

Container grown plants will continue to grow until you plant them, so they'll keep for awhile. But provide adequate light and water.

STARTING YOUR OWN

Some vines (especially rootlet vines) are easy to start from cuttings; others (especially annual varieties) are quick to grow from seed.

Both are inexpensive and cuttings may even be free, if they are taken from your own garden or from an accommodating friend.

VINES FROM CUTTINGS

Some rootlet vines such as wintercreeper, climbing hydrangea, creeping fig, and evergreen ivy root if you merely stick them in the ground. Plant them in the spring from cuttings taken before new leaves have formed.

Use cuttings that are 4 to 6 inches in length, ideally with rootlets growing on the stem. Take two to three times as many cuttings as you need in case some don't grow. Remove any leaves from the lower two thirds of the cutting, and bury that much of the stem in a pot or directly in the ground. If you're planting in a container, use a potting medium—two to three parts perlite mixed with one part peat is excellent.

If you are direct planting, add organic matter or potting mix to the soil and keep the cuttings in indirect light. In full sun, shade them with a light cloth. Keep the cover a few inches away from the cuttings, and keep the soil moist until they root—usually about six to eight weeks.

VINES FROM SEED

Annual vines, such as scarlet runner bean and morning glories, are easy plants to grow from seed. Give them a head start indoors about four weeks before the last expected frost. Plant them in individual pots in potting medium. When they've sprouted, move them to a brightly lighted area (a sunny window, a greenhouse, or under fluorescent lights). As the days warm, set the seedlings outside in indirect sunlight to "harden them off" but take them inside at night. After a week, they're ready for the daytime sun. When the weather is consistently warm and all danger of frost is past, transplant them but take care to disturb the roots as little as possible.

Directly sowing is even easier. For each vine, after the soil has warmed in late spring, plant three to five seeds in each location you've chosen. Keep the soil moist. When the seedings are several inches high, thin all but the strongest in each group.

MAIL ORDER NURSERIES

Gossler Farms Nursery
    1200 Weaver Rd., Springfield, OR 97478
Heronswood Nursery, Ltd.
    7530 288th NE, Kingston, WA 98346
Logee's Greenhouses
    141 North St., Danielson, CT 06239
Louisiana Nursery
    Rt.7, Box 43, Opelousas, LA 70570
Niche Gardens
    1111 Dawson Rd., Chapel Hill, NC 27516
Nichols Garden Nursery
    1190 N. Pacific Hwy., Albany, OR 97321
Shepherd's Garden Seeds
    30 Irene St., Torrington, CT 06790
Thompson & Morgan
    P.O. Box 1308, Jackson, NJ 08527
W. Atlee Burpee & Co.
    300 Park Ave., Warminster, PA 18974
White Flower Farm
    P.O. Box 50, Litchfield, CT 06759

Take cuttings of rootlet vines by pruning off 4- to 6-inch lengths, preferably shoots with small rootlets already growing. Cut just above a bud and then recut the shoot just below its lowest bud.

Bury the lower two-thirds of the cutting in the soil. In full sun, shade it with a light cloth, held a few inches away on stakes or on a frame made from hangers, wire, hardware cloth, or fencing.

Some seeds germinate more quickly if they are soaked overnight before sowing. In most cases, they will dramatically swell in size.

Follow the directions on the seed packet. Loosen the soil, bury the seed slightly, and keep the soil moist until the seedlings germinate.

PLANTING PRIMER

The key to successful growing lies both in selecting varieties appropriate to locations and in good soil preparation and proper planting. Because vines are among the most adaptable to a wide range of soil conditions, you will not normally need to add soil amendments.

PLANTING

Dig the planting hole as deep as the roots and at least twice as wide as the root spread. If you're planting under an established tree, dig the hole only as wide as the root spread.

Prepare and loosen the soil by turning it over with a shovel. Under an established tree, loosen only enough to make a hole for the vine's roots.

Plant container-grown vines at the same depth they grew in the pot. Fill the planting hole with soil and make a rim to hold water.

For bare-root vines, build a mound of soil in the center of the hole and spread out the bare roots over the mound. Pack soil around the roots.

Once the plant is established, use a "nurse stake" to encourage it to grow toward the structure onto which it will climb.

For bare root plants, build a mound of soil in the center of the hole, carefully spread the roots out over the mound, pack soil around the roots, and fill the hole with the remaining soil.

You don't need a mound for container-grown plants, but if their roots are tight and have begun to circle the container, make a vertical cut in the center of the soil mass. Cut about a quarter of the way up; it will encourage the roots to grow straight.

Set the root ball in the hole to the same depth as planted in the container and fill the remainder of the hole with soil.

Finish both kinds of planting with a 6- to 8-inch-high rim of soil at the edge of the root spread; it will direct water to the roots.

Once the plant is established, it may need help in growing toward its structure. Place a "nurse stake" between the vine and its structure; the vine will grow around the stake, and you can train it toward its structure.

WATERING

Newly planted vines need daily watering for the first week. After that, and through the first year, water thoroughly whenever the soil feels dry to the touch. Watch for drooping leaves—they indicate severe stress. Touch the soil above the root area (not the loose fill soil). If it's dry, water it immediately. If it's wet, don't water. You may be watering too much, or the plant may be injured.

FERTILIZING

A slow-release organic fertilizer returns natural ingredients to the soil and insures a steady supply of ingredients as roots develop. Work it into the soil a week before planting, or sprinkle it and water it in. A good general-purpose fertilizer for vines will have a 5-10-5 analysis on its label. If you are trying to encourage flowering, use a "tomato fertilizer" with low Nitrogen.

If your vines are growing satisfactorily, they may not need supplemental fertilizer—certainly not if they're overly vigorous.

PEST CONTROL

Vigorous plants are more resistant to pests and diseases. If a plant is being attacked, first check the soil. Is it too dry or too wet? Is it compacted? If the pest or disease problem persists, consult your garden center, a professional horticulturist, or your county extension office for the proper remedy.

Keep your garden area clean and the weeds pulled. Remove any diseased parts of the vine right away and discard them. Inspect your plants regularly.

VINES IN CONTAINERS: GROWING

Plants growing in containers require more care than those grown in the ground. They need regular watering and periodic fertilization because the container does not provide enough soil for proper moisture and nutrient release. Year-round plants need watering even during the winter whenever the soil is not frozen. The soil needs to be relatively light and must drain well.

PLANTING

Commercial soil mixes are easy to use and work well in containers, but they are usually very low in fertility. You may want to add a small amount of slow-release fertilizer. Soil mixes can also be difficult to moisten. Wet the mix before the soil is put in the container, but do not make it soggy.

Fill the container with your soil mix and plant the vine as discussed on page 42. If the support on which the vine will grow is going to be in the container itself, put it in when you are filling in the soil or after planting, whichever makes more sense. If the vine will be growing on a support outside the pot, use a "nurse stake" to make a temporary bridge from pot to support. Mulch will reduce weeds and the need for frequent watering.

SELECTING A CONTAINER

Most vines require excellent drainage; make sure the container has holes in the bottom to provide it. If the container will be left outside year-round, it should be able to withstand the freezing and thawing of winter. Wood, fiberglass, and concrete containers work well as winter containers. Terra-cotta (clay) pots will generally crack and break apart in freezing weather.

Pots filled with plants and moist soil are very heavy. Consider containers with wheels, or move them on a dolly.

The size of the container is also significant. The larger the better, but if the container will be moved inside for the winter, make sure it's not too heavy to move. Small containers are easier to move but quickly fill with roots and require frequent watering. For either large or small containers drip irrigation systems may make watering easier and reduce wasted water. There are a number of systems available, ranging from low-tech soaker hoses to automated systems. Check with your local garden center or irrigation supplier.

Commercial potting soils are difficult to moisten. Add a small amount of water and mix it into the soil. Repeat until the soil is evenly moist.

After planting, cover the soil with a 1-inch layer of mulch, such as shredded bark, to reduce weeds and retain moisture.

Containers allow vines to be grown where there is no open ground. The container should be attractive and able to withstand weather conditions of the area.

EASY QUICK SUPPORTS

Find a place where you would like a vine, choose a plant, picture what the structure will look like, and you're almost there. But what if the structure doesn't already exist? Don't let that stop you. Be creative. Supports can be as simple as a pole; they don't have to be complex or pricey. Besides, the lack of an existing structure may mean you have just the perfect opportunity to grow vines in an unusual place.

Plant a twining vine on a single bamboo pole or multiply the effect with a series of them. Make tripods of three poles tied at the top; tripods are more stable than single poles. You can buy poles and ready-made tripods from catalogs and garden centers, or cut your own from sturdy saplings.

Arrange strands of wire or string along a wall or hang them from a tree branch or roof. Netting in front of a wall or a wooden fence is easily taken down for painting or other maintenance, and can be rehung when the work is done.

Even a dead tree or a clothesline pole can become an attractive, living sculpture when cloaked in vines.

Sturdy tripods are easy supports to make, and work well for any twining vine. Start with 6- to 8-foot poles, set them 1 foot deep, and tie them together at the top with twine.

TYING CLIMBERS

Rambling roses and other climbers cannot attach themselves to structures. They sprawl on other plants or must be fastened or woven to supports, such as a lattice, steel arch, wrought iron, wire, or string. Tie loosely, or the vine's stem may become girdled as it grows and expands.

For solid surfaces such as walls, attach wire, twine, or string with fasteners. String or twine is easy, but wire is strong and long-lasting. It can hang horizontally or be made into a design. On wood walls, use a screw hook or eye. Special fasteners are sold for use on masonry walls and are either inserted into the wall or are attached by adhesive.

Attach climbers to lattice using flexible fabric. You also can weave the stems of climbers in and out of a lattice structure.

Attach vinyl-coated wires to wood posts or walls with staples or screw eyes and tie climbers to the wire. To paint the wood later, take down the wire and gently bend the climber away from the wall or post.

Pound a masonry fastener into the wall and then bend over the vine's stem to hold it to the brick wall.

Attach wire to the wall and the rose to wire as the rose grows. Choose tie material that will blend in with and be hidden by the climber. Green twine and green "twist-ems" are easily used and inconspicuous.

Large tripods can resemble a teepee and create a feeling of enclosure. They are one of the easiest supports to create. Plant an individual vine on each pole for quick cover.

An individual string or a wire can support a clinging vine, or a scrambling vine can be tied to it. Interesting designs can be patterned by the string.

String netting offers many opportunities to use vines. Hang the netting near a tendril or twining vine and it will soon cover the netting. Hang it in front of a wall or on a tree trunk, or let it form a wall by itself.

Quick structures you buy and set in place, such as an ornamental column or a ready-made arch, give immediate support for twining or rootlet vines. And they can provide beauty even before the vine grows.

A GARDEN LADDER

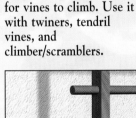

A ladder under eaves is a simple, elegant structure for vines to climb. Use it with twiners, tendril vines, and climber/scramblers.

The ladder stands away from the house, allowing air circulation. It's perfect for houses sided with wood, aluminum, or vinyl.

For an added design detail, project dowels past the posts.

For a wider trellis, join two sets of dowels at a post (top). Use angle braces to attach the trellis posts to the soffit if rafters are enclosed.

The finished ladder with a scrambling vine

HOW TO PRUNE

The rules for pruning vines are similar to the ones for all plants. When pruning is necessary, a general rule applies: Know your plant and its pruning needs and be clear about what you're trying to accomplish.

Pruning will help keep your vines healthy, but it can also rejuvenate them, shape them, encourage flowering or fruiting, and control their growth or remove one that's become a problem. Because of their vigor, most vines are quite forgiving of pruning mistakes and quick to recover. But no matter what your reasons for pruning, be sure to step back from time to time to assess your progress and to keep yourself from being overly zealous.

Here are some general practices you should follow when pruning. Make your cut just above a healthy bud, or at a juncture of two stems. Angle the cut down and away from the bud at 45 degrees (so that sap will drip away from the bud and not cover it). New growth will appear from this bud. Cuts toward the end of a stem encourage new shoots to appear along its length for greater fullness. Removing

stems to the trunk tends to encourage growth at the top of the vine for greater height. You can also cut most vines back to ground level; they will regrow where the cut was made.

Making the cuts is the easy part of vine pruning because the stems are seldom very large. The real challenge is next—removing the shoots you've cut. They are usually entwined among themselves and the structure. Start cutting a stem from the top, removing small sections at a time. Continue until the entire stem is gone. Don't pull out a long, entangled shoot. You may damage other parts of the vine and risk pulling the support apart (or over). Occasionally unwinding a vine stem first makes pruning it off easier.

TIMING

You can prune at any time of the year, but depending on your purpose for pruning, some times are better than others. If you're trying to maximize the bloom of your vines, prune them after they flower. This allows them time to produce buds for the next year's bloom. In general, prune spring bloomers in early summer and summer bloomers in the winter.

Winter is also a good time to do other major pruning—especially on deciduous vines. With the foliage gone, you can see the basic structure of the vine. Any branches you cut but don't remove will look like the rest of the dormant plant. If you prune in the summer and miss a cut shoot or two, the leaves will wilt and detract from the summer beauty of the vine. Cut stems are easier to remove in winter, and any extra clothing you wear to keep warm will protect you from thorny plants like roses.

When shortening a stem, make the pruning cut just above a bud. The bud will develop a vigorous new shoot.

Remove an entire stem by making the cut right at another shoot or at the trunk. This opens up a plant to air circulation and light and helps control growth.

Cut a vine within a foot of the ground to control its growth and/or to rejuvenate it. Such pruning drastically reduces the size of the plant. The new growth at the cut will be well-branched and vigorous.

PRUNING FOR PLANT HEALTH

Healthy vines fend off diseases, and pruning will help keep your vines healthy. It allows light in and air to circulate.

Pruning dead or weak stems allows the plant to direct its energy into producing steady new growth. Start with injured or unhealthy stems. Next prune some of the older shoots—they are less floriferous and more likely to be attacked by pests.

If you have a vigorous vine, start pruning when it's young. As vigorous vines mature, their stems get thicker and harder to cut.

PRUNING TO REJUVENATE

Pruning will bring new life to a plant that's grown old. Hard pruning (to within 6 inches of the ground) will promote fresh growth, and many vines are not harmed by it. It's best to do this in the spring, just after the new growth has begun. Cut the vine back to the main stem or even to within a foot of the ground. This will reduce the space the stems will cover. After hard pruning, work in some balanced fertilizer, organic or inorganic, and add mulch and water.

Hard pruning will also rejuvenate an old vine weakened by overgrowth. Spread the process over three years, taking one third of its oldest stems at a time.

"Cutting back to the bones" removes all the side shoots, leaving only the main stems. This reduces the size of the vine and controls its growth, but retains much of the plant's structure.

Protect yourself. Always wear heavy gloves and know where your hands are before making a cut. Safety glasses or goggles are a must. Leather clothing is optional, but you'll wish you had it if pruning thorny vines.

TOOLS

Pruning is frustrating and even dangerous with the wrong tools. Two or three tools are all you need to prune most vines. Do not buy cheap tools. Invest in high-quality equipment. It will last decades with proper care.

First buy a good pruning shears. It is your most important pruning tool and a good all-around gardening investment. Expect to pay over $40, and buy a scissors-type shears (with two moving blades), not an anvil type. Anvil shears have one moving blade that cuts against a flat surface. They tend to crush branches and do not make clean cuts. Some new models are ergonomically engineered (they require less effort to use) and may be worth the few dollars extra, especially if they will be getting a lot of use. Consider a holster for the shears for carrying them while working. Pruning shears stuck in a pocket can damage clothing and produce deep cuts.

The second tool to acquire is a pruning saw. Buy a small one that either folds (and can go in your pocket) or comes with a holster that you can attach to a belt, making it easy to carry safely in the garden. Make sure it has a good locking device to prevent it from folding on your hand while you are pruning.

The third tool to purchase is a lopper—essentially pruning shears with long handles. It cuts stems that are too large for pruning shears and is easier to use than a saw on some cuts.

Pruning tools are sharp and very dangerous. Prune with leather gloves and eye protection. Safety shoes or boots are a good idea for any gardening work.

A good pair of pruning shears and a pruning saw will handle most pruning cuts. High-quality tools are worth the extra cost and will last for decades.

SHIPSHAPE VINES

Wisterias and some fruiting vines, such as grapes and kiwis, flower on short "spur" shoots. When pruning, avoid removing these flowering spurs, which, with a little experience, are easy to discern.

BEST TIMES TO PRUNE FLOWERING VINES

Actinidia: winter*
Akebia: early summer
Allamanda: winter
Ampelopsis: winter*
Antigonon: winter
Aristolochia: early summer
Bignonia: early summer
Bougainvillea: winter
Campsis: winter
Celastrus: winter*
Clematis: prune after flowering, varies with
    individual species and hybrids
Clitoria: winter
Decumaria: early summer
Dicentra: winter
Eccremocarpus: winter
Euonymus: winter
Gelsemium: early summer
Humulus: winter
Hydrangea: early summer, but leave
    horizontal shoots
Jasminum: early summer
Lagenaria: winter
Lathyrus: winter
Lonicera: generally in winter, but varies
    with species
Mandevilla: winter
Passiflora: winter
Polygonum: winter
Rosa: usually done in winter, but spring-
    bloomers could be done in early summer
Schizophragma: early summer
Solanum: winter
Stephanotis: winter
Trachelospermum: winter
Vitis: winter*
Wisteria: early summer
* These vines are grown for fruit; major
pruning is done in winter, but some pruning
to reduce growth is done in the summer.

Much has been written about when to prune for optimal bloom. The simplest rule is this—prune after flowering. This gives the plant time to grow and produce flower buds for the following season.

Spring-blooming vines flower on "old wood" stems. These are stems that have grown the previous summer. Prune spring bloomers within a month after their flowers appear.

Most summer bloomers flower on "new wood"—stems that have grown in the same season. Prune them in the winter when the flower is dormant.

New-wood vines are fairly easy to detect—look for slender, flexible flower stems and smooth skin. But if you make a mistake, the worst that can happen is the vine will skip one flower season.

PRUNING FOR FRUITING

Since fruit comes from flowers, pruning for fruit is the same as pruning for flowers. Most fruit vines, such as grapes and kiwis, bloom in the spring on old wood and ripen in the fall. Prune them in the winter for growth control and to improve the quality of the fruit by reducing quantity.

Both grapes and kiwis produce flowers (and thus fruits) on short, stubby shoots called spurs. When winter pruning, don't remove too many of these spur shoots. You need to leave enough flower buds to produce a good crop.

During the summer, you can prune to shape the plants and to reduce the growth of exceptionally long shoots. Inspect before you summer prune. Look for long shoots beyond the fruits and spurs. Cut the long shoots back to a leaf or two beyond the developing fruit. You'll neaten the plant and keep the shade for the developing fruit.

Reducing the size of a grape vine will promote the growth of fewer, but higher quality, fruit.

PRUNING TO SHAPE

Left untended, vines can become unruly; as elements in a planned design they can be wild and free-flowing creatures. With careful pruning, they become more refined. They branch quickly and provide more rapid results than most trees and shrubs and thus are excellent subjects for specialized uses, such as espaliers and standards (treelike forms with bare trunks).

Perform major pruning for shape in the winter when the framework of deciduous vines is easiest to see. Do the biggest cuts first, pruning back to the main stem. Then finish by pruning back the remaining side shoots (where necessary) to just above a bud. Vigorous vines that need regular pruning to control size include anemone clematis, sweet autumn clematis, wisteria, and akebia.

Summer is the time for minor shaping. Prune back shoots that are growing beyond the framework you have established. Cut back to a stem or to just above a bud or a leaf (buds form in the leaf axils). With young plants, encourage branching by pinching out the growing point where you want it to branch.

ESPALIER

Use wires or wood to establish the pattern along which the vine will be trained. Plant a young vine at the base and, in the first year, train as much growth as possible along the framework.

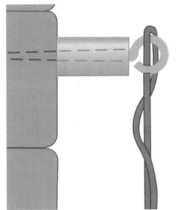

As the vine grows, encourage it along the framework by tying the young shoots or simply wrapping them around the wires. Where branching is needed, pinch or cut the shoot during the summer to just above a leaf. Shear or cut off shoots that grow beyond the framework.

Many styles of espalier are possible with vines— horizontal or vertical straight lines, angles, diamonds, hearts, and triangles.

HONEYSUCKLE STANDARD

Start with a young vine and a stake that is long and strong enough to support the final tree form. Train a single shoot upward, tying it to the stake and removing all side shoots.

Once the stem has reached the desired height, pinch off the growing shoot. The plant will send out new shoots. Let each grow a new leaf and pinch again to encourage bushy growth.

Shape the top growth into a ball and your standard is ready for display.

KEEP VINES UNDER CONTROL

Sooner or later, there's a good chance you'll be faced with a vine that needs some severe discipline—or even removal. Pruning is the best way to both control or remove vines, and the process for each is slightly different.

PRUNING FOR CONTROL

If you want to reduce the size of the vine significantly, then winter pruning is the answer. To merely keep the growth of the vine in tow, you need to prune in midsummer.

To winter prune, cut the vine back to its major shoots (its "bones") or to within a foot or two of the ground. Before you cut back to the main stems, first determine where they are (they're easier to see in the winter). The main stems on a twining vine will be woven on the structure. Cut all shoots that are sticking out from it. With tendril and rootlet vines, cut the plant back to its trunk and side shoots.

Cutting to the ground is easy. Find where the vine comes out of the soil and make the cut within 1 or 2 feet of the ground. Some

Remove a vine in pieces, starting from the top down. This reduces the risk to the structure or plant on which the vine is growing. Yanking large, uncut vines can bring down an arbor and result in damage or injury.

Vines that have rooted onto walls are a challenge to remove. The vine will tend to break while you are pulling it, and it will be almost impossible to remove the rootlets. Wait until winter, so you will not have to look at wilted leaves.

Control the growth of vigorous vines by cutting them to the ground in the winter.

gardeners cut it off right at the ground. If the plant is alive and healthy, it will resprout at the cut.

Such winter pruning reduces the size of the plant and in most cases will give you enough control for a year. However, if the vine is exceedingly vigorous and/or it is too big for its structure, summer pruning may also be needed. Summer pruning is primarily cutting back individual shoots. These stick out from the plant and are long and straggly. Cut them back to another branch or to just above a leaf. This will neaten the vine and reduce its jungle look. Prune by midsummer (mid- to late July in most of the country) to allow the plant time to harden off before autumn frost.

Vigorous vines that need regular pruning to control size include anemone clematis, sweet autumn clematis, wisteria, and akebia.

REMOVING VINES

Some vines can shade out and strangle other plants. Large ones can overwhelm structures, despite your best efforts to match the vine to its support. In such cases, you may have to remove the vine, and you have several options.

You can dig out the vine and its roots, cut one or more major stems of the vine, or cut the vine to the ground and let it resprout under a different training regimen. Each option is best done in winter when the vine will be dormant or looks as if it is going dormant. (It can be difficult to remove all the stems, and in the summer telltale wilted leaves will hang on for the rest of the season.) If any parts of the vine are left, they will not be noticed and can be left to decompose. In the dormant season, it is also easier to distinguish the vine from its support.

When removing a vine from a structure or plant, be very careful. Most will be too big to pull out at once, and doing so may damage the support or the plant. Work from the top down and remove the vine in pieces, as gently as possible.

TROUBLESHOOTING CHECKLIST

- ☐ Surface of structure in poor condition
- ☐ Vines rooting into wood
- ☐ Vines growing under shingles or siding
- ☐ Twining vines on trees
- ☐ Vines overwhelming a tree or other plants
- ☐ A vigorous vine planted on a small structure or in a small space

POISON IVY

Poison ivy has outstanding red fall color, and female plants bear complementary white berries. It also can send people to the hospital with skin reactions. It endangers the lungs and lives of people who inadvertently burn it and inhale the smoke. It is not a plant to have around the home.

If possible, get rid of poison ivy while it is still a seedling. Wear gloves while pulling out seedlings and discard gloves and plants in the trash or a compost pile. The dangerous oils will slowly break down and become harmless. Be sure not to touch the outside of your gloves when removing them. Herbicides can be sprayed on the foliage of younger plants to kill them during the summer.

Larger plants are more difficult to deal with. Wear gloves and protective clothing, and cut trunks of large vines at ground level. Paint the cut with an herbicide (your local garden center can suggest one). If done in winter, there are no wilted leaves to look at. Leave the old vine in place and wait several months before removing it. Do not burn it.

Poison ivy has several characteristics that will help you recognize it. There are three leaflets that turn brilliant red in winter. The bare winter stems are whitish gray and ascend at the tips. Female plants bear clusters of white berries in autumn.

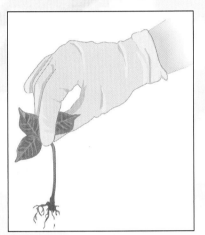

Poison ivy seedlings have the distinctive grouping of three leaflets and, at this stage, are easy to pull, roots and top. Wear gloves and avoid any contact with the leaves, stems, and roots. Dispose of the plant and the gloves in the trash (do not burn them).

Pulling a large vine off a tree will expose you to the irritating oil from the leaves and stems. Instead, during the winter cut the vine near its base and paint the cut with an herbicide. Leave the vine in the tree for several months or more to allow the harmful oils to dissipate. The dead vine can eventually be removed but should not be burned.

QUICK REMOVAL WITH NETTING

String or wire netting makes temporary removal of vines easy. If the wall behind needs painting or other maintenance, just take the netting off its hooks and lay both netting and vine on the ground. After the maintenance is done, rehang the netting. An additional advantage is that the netting can be several inches away from the wall, allowing air to circulate. Twiners and tendril-type vines are the best kinds to use on netting.

Netting allows for easy removal of vines from structures that need maintenance.

SELECTION AND GROWING GUIDE

Vines add color and privacy to contemporary gardens. This rose completely covers a fence with brilliant blossoms, yet entices one to see what is on the other side.

The following guide to our recommended vines is full of information you'll need to make gratifying gardening decisions and grow healthy, beautiful vines. This isn't an encyclopedia of every vine known, but instead a carefully selected list of the most garden-worthy vines that are readily available.

At the beginning of each listing you'll find an easy-to-browse summary of key features, growth rate and climbing habit, and hardiness (you can locate your zone in the USDA Hardiness Zone Map on page 92). Remember that these hardiness listings are estimates only, because many factors, not just the average low winter temperature of your region, determine the success of a plant.

The summaries are followed by descriptions of the plants, their uses, and tips for supports, placement, and care. Recommended cultivars and species are also described.

The selection guide is alphabetized by scientific name, although you will also find a common name listed for each vine. There are often many common names for the same plant, differing from region to region, but there is only one scientific name, agreed upon worldwide. Scientific names are made up of at least two Latin words. The first name is the genus—a group of plants that share certain characteristics, such as similar flowers. The second name is the specific name, or species. There are often many species within a genus.

A cultivar name often follows as a third part of a scientific name, and is always set apart in single quotation marks. Cultivars have specific, usually superior, differences from the species. A hybrid results from the crossing of two plant species, and is noted with a multiplication sign (×). Species generally come true from seed, while cultivars and hybrids usually need to be propagated asexually (for example, by cuttings or grafts) to retain their desirable characteristics.

Paul's Himalayan Musk rose adds shade and luscious color to an open pergola.

ACTINIDIA DELICIOSA

Kiwi

- Deciduous; climbs by twining
- Bold foliage, delicious fruit
- Vigorous; grows 10 to 15 feet per year; pruning may be needed to contain growth
- Zones 7 to 9

USES: *Actinidia deliciosa* (formerly *A. chinensis*) is the kiwi of the grocery store. The distinctive green-fleshed, edible fruit is about the size of an egg.

In gardens, kiwi is grown for ornamental foliage as well as fruit. The leaves are large, bold, and very attractive. Kiwi grown for foliage is hardy to zone 6, where it will die to the ground each winter but resprout from the base. However, since fruit develops only on the previous year's growth, it is difficult to grow this vine for fruit north of zone 7. Kiwi's bold texture contrasts well with fine-textured plants, such as the false cypresses (*Chamaecyparis*). Native to China.

SITING AND CARE: Kiwi tolerates both sun and shade, but needs full sun for fruiting. Moisture needs are moderate, but good drainage is important. You'll need male and female plants for fruiting.

Grow kiwi on wires and strong arbors. It has few pest problems.

RECOMMENDED CULTIVARS: 'Blake' is self-fruiting; 'Vincent' is a fruiting cultivar that is good for warm areas; 'Hayward' is commercially grown for its fruit; and 'Tomuri', which is male, has attractive red stems and dark green leaves.

Hayward kiwi is one of the major cultivars grown commercially for its fruit.

ACTINIDIA ARGUTA

Siberian gooseberry

- Delicious, bite-size fruit
- Deciduous; climbs by twining
- Vigorous; grows up to 15 feet per year
- Zones 4 to 8

USES: This hardy vine enables gardeners in northern climates to enjoy much of the beauty and delicious flavor of kiwi. Although its grape-size, hairless fruits are individually smaller, they are quite delicious, and production can be heavy. The leaves are bold and hairless, but one third the size of kiwi's. The bark becomes very attractive with age, peeling and revealing gray and brown underbark. Flowers are white and fragrant but not showy. Native to eastern Asia.

SITING AND CARE: This vine tolerates sun or shade but fruits best in full sun. Its moisture needs are moderate, but it should have good drainage. Pruning may be needed to contain its vigorous growth, and both male and female flowers are needed to set fruit. This vine rarely has pest problems.

RECOMMENDED CULTIVARS: Selections include the cultivars 'Ananasnaya', very hardy and vigorous, with large clusters of small fruit; and 'Issai', self-fruiting.

Siberian gooseberry ('Ananasnaya') has small but tasty fruit and attractive bark.

ACTINIDIA KOLOMIKTA

Kolomikta vine

- Leaves mottled with blotches of pink, green, and white
- Deciduous; climbs by twining
- Grows about 5 feet per year
- Zones 3 to 8

USES: The bold, tri-colored leaves of this species distinguish it from all other vines. The pink coloration is strongest in direct sunlight. Flowers are fragrant but not showy.

The foliage is beautiful when matched with purple and rust tones such as brick and brownstone. Try combining this vine with purple-leaved plants, such as purpleleaf sand cherry or 'Forest Pansy' redbud, or paint its supporting structure purple.

Most plants sold are male and thus do not produce fruit. Females produce fruit resembling those of *A. arguta*. Native to eastern Asia.

SITING AND CARE: Kolomikta tolerates sun and shade, but performs best in light shade. It needs moderate moisture, and must have good drainage. Shade the roots with a small shrub or with perennials and let the vine climb. This is a fine choice to grow on sturdy trellises and even small trees. It is rarely bothered by pests.

RECOMMENDED CULTIVARS: Selections include 'Arctic Beauty', with slightly smaller leaves, which open purple and mature to a mixture of white, pink, and green; and 'Arnold Arboretum', a female selection bearing small, edible fruit.

Kolomikta vine foliage has blotches of pink and white, backed by green.

The distinctive flowers and five-parted leaves of Akebia quinata

AKEBIA QUINATA

Akebia, Chocolate vine

■ Beautiful leaves and chocolate-colored flowers
■ Deciduous, climbs by twining
■ Vigorous; grows 10 to 15 feet per year
■ Zones 5 to 9

USES: Grown mostly for its refined, lovely foliage, akebia also produces subtle flowers that are showy up close, so plant it near a walkway where you are sure to pass it. The flowers appear early as the new leaves are unfurling, and they remain for several weeks. The dark green leaves are quite beautiful: Five oval leaflets stay until very late fall, when they turn brown and then drop. Plants do not usually produce fruit unless several are present for cross-pollination.

The fleshy unattractive fruit can send seedlings into the wild. Birds like to nest in akebia, and it tends to be pest resistant. Try growing akebia with other spring-blooming plants with pink flowers, such as cherries. Native to eastern Asia.

SITING AND CARE: Akebia thrives in sun or shade. It tolerates a fair amount of moisture but not flooding. Akebia twines around arbors, trellises, chain link, wrought iron, and posts. Make sure the structures are strong because this vine is very vigorous. It grows quickly once established and, unless given a lot of space, needs pruning two or three times during the summer. Blooms are produced on old wood, so heavy pruning should be done in late spring, just after flowering. It also sends out horizontal shoots which can root and climb up neighboring flower or shrub beds, becoming quite weedy. In lawn areas, the mower easily controls them.

RECOMMENDED CULTIVARS: There is a white-flowered selection, called 'Alba', and 'Variegata', a variegated cultivar. The variegated plant is not very vigorous. Use it where you want an accent plant with yellow and green leaves—in front of a dark house or near a group of dark evergreens. 'Rosea' has lavender flowers; 'Shirobana' has fragrant white flowers.

Golden trumpet is an excellent choice for containers.

ALLAMANDA CATHARTICA

Golden trumpet, Allamanda

■ Showy yellow flowers all summer
■ Evergreen tropical, but excellent to grow as an annual in the North
■ Sprawls, so needs to be tied or woven onto supports or grown on other plants
■ Grows 6 to 8 feet in a summer (more vigorous in the South)
■ Zone 10

USES: Large, showy golden yellow flowers with a background of dark green foliage make this a knockout plant in the summer garden. It is a good, easy-to-grow annual vine in the North, and it produces enough flowers to justify its one-season of growth. Try it with other golden yellow flowers, or with purples and blues for vibrant contrast. Native to South America.

SITING AND CARE: Grow golden trumpet in full sun after danger of frost has past. It needs ample moisture but good drainage. Tie golden trumpet on arbors and pillars or weave it in fencing (including chain link) and trellises. It does beautifully in a large container. North of zone 10, discard golden trumpet in the fall or overwinter it in a sunny indoor spot. Prune it back hard before taking inside or prune just before planting out in early summer to encourage dense growth.

RECOMMENDED CULTIVARS: 'Flore Pleno' has golden double flowers.

AMPELOPSIS BREVIPEDUNCULATA

Porcelain vine

■ Unusual fruit with a porcelain finish; profuse, weedy, and difficult to control
■ Deciduous; climbs by tendrils and twining
■ Vigorous; grows 10 feet in one summer
■ Zones 5 to 9

USES: This is a heartbreak vine, lovely but weedy. Flowers are small, greenish, and inconspicuous, but fruit is beautiful, with variously colored white, blue, and purple berries resembling exquisite porcelain. Fall color is a weak yellow. Seedlings must be vigilantly removed to keep them from taking over. Native to eastern Asia.

SITING AND CARE: Porcelain vine grows in sun or shade and tolerates drought. Grow on chain link and large arbors.
RECOMMENDED CULTIVARS AND RELATED SPECIES: The cultivar 'Elegans' has variegated leaves flushed white, yellow, and pink with touches of green. You'll be able to identify its seedlings as you pull them because they are variegated, too.

If you must plant this genus, try a cousin, the pepper vine (*Ampelopsis arborea*). It is native to the Southeast, is hardy in zones 7 to 9, and has purple fruit. However, plant with caution: Pepper vine can also be weedy.

Variegated porcelain vine, 'Elegans'

ANTIGONON LEPTOPUS

Coral vine, Confederate vine

■ Coral pink flowers in late summer
■ Deciduous; climbs by tendrils
■ Vigorous; grows 10 to 15 feet in a season
■ Zones 9 to 10 (will survive in Zone 8 but dies to the ground in winter)

USES: Completely covering itself in rosy pink flowers, coral vine is a spectacular sight late in the season, when the showy effect of other plants is at a premium. It's easy to grow and tolerant of difficult conditions. Native to Mexico.
SITING AND CARE: This vine grows well in sunny spots and tolerates drought and hot, dry climates. Coral vine is very vigorous and should be planted on lattice, chain link fence or on other plants. Cut it back hard each spring (repeat in early summer if necessary) to control airy and profuse growth.
RECOMMENDED CULTIVARS: 'Album' has white flowers; 'Baja Red', has deep rose-red flowers.

Coral vine blooming in late summer

ARISTOLOCHIA MACROPHYLLA (DURIOR)

Dutchman's pipe

■ Bold foliage and unique flowers
■ Deciduous; climbs by twining
■ Vigorous; grows 10 to 15 feet in a season
■ Zones 4 to 7

USES: This is one of the boldest-textured vines, with large (to 12 inches wide) and long, rounded, dark green leaves. The flowers of Dutchman's pipe are the source of its common name. These fantastic, purplish brown flowers do look like macabre pipes. They are small and hidden by the leaves, so plant it in a location that you will see from behind, as on a porch or next to a window. Native to the eastern United States.
SITING AND CARE: Easy and adaptable, this is a vine that is virtually maintenance free. It grows in sun or shade, needs adequate moisture, and is generally untroubled by pests. Grow it on posts, arbors, chain link fences, or screened porches. Its flowers are a favorite food of the rare pipe vine swallowtail butterfly larvae.

Dutchman's pipe (at left, a close-up of the flower)

Climbing snapdragon on netting

ASARINA

Climbing snapdragon

■ Annual grown for summer bloom; great for containers
■ Climbs by twining and by wrapping leaf stalk around objects
■ Grows to 8 feet in one summer
■ Can be perennial zones 9 to 10

USES: This cousin of the snapdragon is a pretty climber, with red-purple flowers resembling snapdragons and small, fine-textured leaves. Perennial in subtropical areas, it's grown as an annual

north of zone 9. Native to Mexico and the southwestern United States.
SITING AND CARE: Plant climbing snapdragons in full sun with moderate moisture and good drainage. It is not overly vigorous and tends to be well mannered in the garden. Let it climb over other plants or scramble up chain link fences. Mix it with flowers and leaves with purple tones. It is generally untroubled by pests.
RECOMMENDED CULTIVARS: Two selections of *Asarina scandens* are 'Mystic Pink', with pink flowers, and 'Joan Loraine', with purple flowers that have a white throat. Other related cultivars are 'Bride's White', with white flowers; 'Jewel Mixed', with pink flowers and arrow-shaped leaves; 'Pink Ice', with pink flowers and triangular leaves.

The tubular flowers of cross vine are attractive to hummingbirds.

BIGNONIA CAPREOLATA

Cross vine

■ Reddish-orange fragrant flowers
■ Semievergreen to evergreen; climbs by tendrils with adhesive discs
■ Grows quickly, 10 to 20 feet per year
■ Southern part of zones 6 to 9

USES: From late spring well into summer this Southerner provides a massive, long-season display of red-orange flowers. They look great against brick or tan walls, and the color complements strong purples. The species is fragrant, although most cultivars seem to lack any scent. The tubular blossoms are very

attractive to hummingbirds. The shiny, dark green leaves of cross vine turn reddish purple in the South but in colder climates tend to brown by the end of winter. Native to southeastern United States.
SITING AND CARE: Cross vine grows best in soil that has ample amounts of organic matter and moderate moisture. It tolerates heavy shade but blooms best in full sun. Protect the leaves from winter winds. Its tendrils wrap around other plants, onto netting and chain link. The adhesive discs at the tips of the tendrils allow the plant to climb tree trunks and masonry surfaces. Cross vine is little troubled by pests.
RECOMMENDED CULTIVARS: 'Atrosanguinea' has reddish purple flowers. 'Tangerine Beauty' is clear orange. 'Velcyll' is orange on the outside and yellow on the inside. It is hardier than 'Tangerine Beauty'.

Long-lasting bougainvillea flowers scramble over this arched entryway.

BOUGAINVILLEA GLABRA

Bougainvillea, Paper flower

■ Spectacular flower bracts
■ Evergreen; sprawls, so must be tied
■ Rampant growth; 20' per year
■ Zones 9 to 10; often grown as an annual or a container plant in the North

USES: This is one of the most famous of the subtropical vines. It is grown as a greenhouse flower in the North and is popular outdoors in warm climates as a perennial. The plants produce flowers

whenever the weather is hot. The bracts surrounding the flowers provide the real show of color and remain attractive for up to a month. The colors are strong and often best surrounded by the green of other plants. Native to South America.
SITING AND CARE: Bougainvillea grows well in full sun with moderate moisture and good drainage. Watch out for the thorny stems and stand back as it grows! Grow it on an arbor or spilling over a wall. Aphids can be a problem.
RECOMMENDED CULTIVARS: There are many cultivars (some are selections of the hybrid *B.* x *buttiana*), ranging in color from flamboyant pink to orange, yellow, and white. 'Raspberry Ice' has white and green leaves with red flowers.

CAMPSIS RADICANS

Trumpet vine, Trumpet creeper

- Bold, showy flowers summer into fall
- Deciduous; climbs by twining and rootlets on the stem
- Zones 4 to 9

USES: This is a boisterous plant. Big (2-inch wide), bold, orange flowers from July until September seem to shout that they will not be ignored. Hummingbirds will visit these blossoms regularly. However, campsis spreads by suckers and seeds into other garden areas and often becomes a weed. Its flowers are so large they can be messy to clean up if they drop onto vehicles, furniture, or paving. Give them lots of space in an area where bold orange will be welcome. Native to southeastern United States.

SITING AND CARE: Trumpet vine grows in sun or shade, but flowers best in full sun. It can tolerate dry or wet conditions and is generally pest free. Since trumpet vine is such a vigorous grower, plant on masonry, sturdy posts, or chain link fences.

RECOMMENDED CULTIVARS, RELATED SPECIES: 'Crimson Trumpet' has large red flowers; 'Flava', golden yellow. *C. grandiflora* (Chinese trumpet vine) is hardy to zones 7 to 9 and has red or orange-pink flowers. *C. × tagliabuana* 'Madame Galen' is hardy to zones 6 to 9, with large, red-orange flowers.

Trumpet vine is fast growing and covers itself in showy flowers from midsummer until early autumn. Hummingbirds love it.

CELASTRUS SCANDENS

American bittersweet

- Fabulous display of fruits in autumn
- Deciduous; climbs by twining
- Vigorous; grows 10 to 15 feet a year
- Southern part of zones 3 to 8

USES: The red-orange fruit of bittersweet symbolizes autumn. The flowers are small and easily missed by all but the most dedicated plant sleuths. American bittersweet is especially showy on an evergreen background and is generally healthy. The plant is rare and endangered in much of the East and should not be collected from the wild. Its Asian cousin (*C. orbiculatus*) is very invasive and weedy, often found in natural areas where it smothers and kills trees by girdling. *C. scandens* is native to North America.

SITING AND CARE: American bittersweet grows in sun or shade, fruiting best in the sun. It tolerates a wide range of moisture. Cut stems dry well and remain showy all winter. Plant American bittersweet on large posts, strong trellises, and chain link fences. Include one male plant for every two or three females to assure fruit production.

RELATED SPECIES: The American species differs from Asian by having clusters of fruits only at the tips of the shoots. Oriental bittersweet produces its fruits in clusters on side shoots.

American bittersweet has extremely showy autumn fruit.

Top to bottom: Niobe, Mrs. P.B. Troth, Ville de Lyon and Henryi clematis hybrids

CLEMATIS HYBRIDS

Clematis (Large-flowered hybrids)

■ Stunning displays of large flowers and showy seed heads
■ Deciduous; climbs by wrapping leaf stems around a structure, and by twining
■ Most grow 5 to 8 feet per year
■ Most are hardy in zones 4 or 5 southward to zone 8

USES: These big-blossomed babies always draw raves from guests. Unfortunately, clematis have an unwarranted reputation for being finicky and a challenge to prune.

Because the large-flowered hybrid clematis are generally restrained in habit and light weight, they are favorite choices to grow on other blooming plants such as shrubs, small trees, and other vines. Try growing one on another plant, such as a spring-blooming tree peony. Match the colors; plant a pink clematis on a pink shrub, or for a purple planting, use summer-blooming, purple-flowered Jackman clematis (*Clematis × jackmanii*) on beautyberry (*Callicarpa bodinieri* cv. 'Profusion') or crimson pygmy barberry. The clematis blooms during the summer and then the beautyberry takes over with purple fruit in the fall. Plant a blue or purple-flowered clematis next to an artemesia. The clematis will lounge all summer in the lush silvery leaves.

SITING AND CARE: Clematis grows best with cool roots and leaves exposed to the sun, so plant the roots in the shade and train the vine to grow into the light. Bury 2 or 3 inches of the stem; it will send out its own roots, increasing the odds of survival. Plant the vine on the north side of a shrub, tree, or tree stump. It will grow up into the sunshine. Plant it behind a trellis and let the vine grow through the supports. It will eventually shade its own roots. Heavy mulching with bark or wood chips also helps keep the roots cool. Good drainage and moderate moisture are important. Clematis is generally little troubled by pests, but wilt can be a problem. If the plant wilts soon after planting, don't panic. It will probably resprout from the base (this is the reason you planted it deeply). Keep it moist (but don't flood it). Additional balanced fertilizer each spring will help maintain or increase its vigor.

Clematis climbs by wrapping the stems of its leaves around a structure or plant, as well as by twining, and grows well on netting, chain link, and light trellises. Choose an attractive structure because these deciduous vines will not hide it in the winter.

The main reasons to prune a clematis are to control growth, to encourage flowering, and to remove dead stems. The plant will show you when and what to prune. Some clematis die back almost to the ground every winter. If yours does, wait till new growth starts in the spring and remove everything dead. If the plant doesn't die back and is not terribly big, don't bother pruning it at all. To encourage it to grow from the base, cut it off about 6 inches from ground level.

Prune after blooming. If it blooms in the spring, prune by midsummer. Winter pruning will remove flower buds. Plants that bloom in the summer produce flowers on the current season's growth. Prune these anytime during the winter. Pruning after new growth starts will delay or prevent flowering.

Just to make life interesting, some of the cultivars start blooming on old wood and then continue to bloom on the new growth. With these plants, avoid pruning except to shape the plant. If it becomes overgrown, cut back hard in winter.

RECOMMENDED CULTIVARS: The following is a small sampling of the many cultivars available: 'Candida' with white flowers, yellow centers; 'Nelly Moser' has pinkish flowers with dark pink bands. 'Comtesse de Bouchaud' has 5-inch-wide, silvery rose flowers all summer long and blooms on new wood.

C. × jackmanii produces violet-purple flowers on new wood in early summer and sporadically throughout the summer.

'General Sikorski' has bluish lavender flowers; 'Henryi', white; 'H.F. Young', large, Wedgwood-blue flowers; 'Miss Bateman', creamy white flowers with reddish centers; 'Niobe' has deep ruby flowers with yellow centers and blooms in late spring and into the summer on new wood. 'Pink Fantasy' is pink; 'Proteus', double flowers that look like mauve peonies; 'Ramona', large and lavender-blue; 'Sugar Candy', pink with a deeper pink stripe and tolerant of partial shade; 'Sunset', large, deep red flowers; 'Ville de Lyon', red flowers; 'Madame le Coultre', white flowers; 'Mrs. Cholmondeley', bluish-purple flowers, and grows to 20 feet.

Vyvyan Pennell

Ville de Lyon

Perle d'Azur

Mrs. George Jackman

Niobe

Lady Northcliffe

Blue Moon

Fireworks

Moonlight

Kacper

Alice Fisk

Nelly Moser

Clematis Madame Baron Veillard

Duchess of Edinburgh

Warsaw Nike

Allanah

**Clematis alpina
'Frances Rivis'**

**Clematis viticella
'Purpurea Plena
Elegans'**

CLEMATIS

Clematis, species

- Beautiful small flowers on vigorous plants
- Climbs by wrapping leaves around a structure
- Vigor and nativity varies among the species
- Hardiness varies with the species

USES: Species clematis are less well-known than their large-flowered hybrid cousins, but they are no less beautiful. Many produce large clusters of small flowers only once during the growing season. Some are quite fragrant and some have attractive seed heads.

Cultural requirements (see pages 58 and 59) are the same as for the large-flowered hybrids, except many of the species tolerate shade.

RECOMMENDED SPECIES: *C. armandii* (Armand clematis), (zones 7 to 9) is an evergreen Chinese species with abundant, showy white, fragrant flowers above shiny, dark green leaves. It blooms in early spring on old wood. It tolerates sun or light shade. *C. cirrhosa* (zones 8 to 9) is also evergreen with drooping, creamy white flowers appearing in fall and winter.

Clematis × *durandii* (zones 5 to 8) is a beautiful hybrid that cannot climb on its own. Weave it through other plants or tie it to support structures. It has deep violet flowers produced in summer on new wood. Train it to grow up through an upright yew or through a purple-leaved smokebush (zones 5 to 8). It is best in full sun.

Grow pink anemone clematis, *C. montana* var. *rubens* (zones 5 to 8) for a vanilla-scented profusion of pink flowers in the spring. The new foliage of this Chinese plant is tinged bronze. Though dainty in appearance, the plant is vigorous enough to cover an entire wall (netting or string is needed). It is very beautiful against brick or a gray stone. It tolerates light shade but is best in full sun. The species (*C. montana*) is rarely available but has white flowers. 'Tetrarose' and 'Mayleen' have larger pink flowers. *C. montana* var. *wilsonii* blooms a week or so later than others with twisted, cream-colored flowers.

The golden clematis species, *C. tangutica* and *C. orientalis* (zones 3 to 8) have yellow flowers in summer and are native to Asia. The flowers point downward, resembling golden bells. Soon after flowering, the plants are covered in attractive feathery, silver seed heads. Grow in full sun. The cultivars 'Bill Mackenzie' and 'Radar Love' have large flowers.

Clematis terniflora (formerly known as *C. paniculata*, *C. maximowicziana*, and *C. dioscoreifolia*. Zones 4 to 9) is the sweet autumn clematis. This plant has had many name changes. You may find it under any of the scientific names listed, but most nurseries simply call it *Clematis paniculata*. Grow this Japanese climber for its late summer profusion of fragrant, small flowers that cover it in a froth of white. Feathery seeds cover the plant following bloom. Warning: It is extremely vigorous! Grow in sun or shade (it blooms best in the sun). It tends to seed itself and become weedy.

Clematis texensis, scarlet clematis, (zones 4 to 8) is a Texas native with fascinating bottle like, deep pink flowers and grayish green leaves. The flowers are not large but definitely attract attention. Plant near a walkway so that flowers are visible. It blooms in mid summer to autumn on new shoots. Have it climb a shiny-leaved evergreen, such as cherry laurel, an evergreen viburnum, or red-tipped photinia. Plant it in full sun for best bloom. 'Gravetye Beauty' has crimson red flowers that are more erect and open than the species. 'Duchess of Albany' has beautiful deep pink flowers that are more open and upright.

Clematis virginiana, Italian clematis, (zones 3 to 7) is the American virgin's bower, native to eastern North America. It is similar in effect to sweet autumn clematis, although less showy in bloom and less vigorous. Its small white flowers appear in late summer and early fall, in sun or shade.

Clematis viticella (zones 5 to 7), blooms on new wood in summer and fall, with nodding flowers in colors ranging from blue to purple to rose-purple, and small, neat leaves. This southern European native is moderately vigorous; early spring pruning encourages branching for a fuller plant. It is the perfect size for growing on a small tree or arbor. Try it on a paperbark maple, a pink rose, or an upright yew; in sun or light shade. 'Betty Corning' flowers over a long period with deep blue blossoms. 'Etoile Violette' has large, dark violet flowers over a longer period than the species. The alpine clematis, *Clematis alpina* (zones 6 to 8) survives to zone 4 with snow cover and has bell-shaped flowers that are bluish violet. It is not very vigorous and blooms in spring on old wood.

Clematis montana var. rubens

Clematis montana *Freda*

Clematis alpina *Willy*

Clematis texensis *'Duchess of Albany'*

Clematis viticella *'Venosa Violacea'*

Clematis texensis *'Gravetye Beauty'*

Clematis tangutica

Clematis texensis

Clematis armandii

Clematis terniflora

Clematis macropetala

Clematis tangutica *'Kugotia' (Golden Tiara™)*

The vibrant blue of **Clitoria ternatea**

CLITORIA TERNATEA

Blue pea

■ Vibrant late summer flowers
■ Evergreen; scrambles, needs to be tied
■ Grows 10 to 15 feet per season
■ Zone 10; usually grown as an annual

USES: Clear blue pealike flowers with a white and yellow center bloom from midsummer until fall. Gardeners north of zone 10 grow this vine as an annual, starting new plants by seed each summer. Use it for quick effect and a long season of bloom. The blue shows up well against gray walls, silver-leaved plants, and weathered wood. Blue pea is an evergreen perennial in the tropics, and can be overwintered indoors in colder climates. It is generally problem-free. Native to Asia.

SITING AND CARE: Plant in full sun. This vine needs lots of water and good drainage.

RECOMMENDED CULTIVARS: 'Blue Sails' and 'Semi-double' have deep blue semidouble (extra petals) flowers.

The bold flowers of cup-and-saucer vine

COBAEA SCANDENS

Cup-and-saucer vine, Cathedral bells

■ Quick growth and showy green-purple flowers
■ Climbs by tendrils
■ Vigorous; grows up to 15 feet in one season
■ Zones 9 to 10; usually grown as an annual

USES: Use this generally healthy vine where you want quick foliage cover and showy flowers. Consider using it while waiting for slower perennial vines to become established. Use it with gray- and silver-colored foliage and materials. The lower portion of the flower resembles a saucer and the upper portion a cup. The honey-scented flowers open greenish and turn a deep purple. Native to Mexico.

SITING AND CARE: Plant seed or seedlings of cup-and-saucer Vine when weather has turned hot in full sun with moderate moisture and good drainage.

RECOMMENDED CULTIVARS: 'Alba' is white flowered and wonderful in areas frequented at night.

An arbor featuring ornamental gourds at eye height

CUCURBITA PEPO

Ornamental gourd

■ Fast growing, with very decorative fruit
■ Annual; climbs by tendrils
■ Vigorous; depending on cultivar, can grow 20 feet in a summer

USES: Warty hardhead, ladle, scoop, odd-finger, bell, pear, apple, and spoon gourds are some of the names applied to the fruit of this species.

Most of the fruit dries well and can be displayed long into winter, with colors a mixture of oranges, yellows, rusts, and greens. The flowers are golden in color. Large leaves, covered with stiff hairs, are bold in texture. Plant them anywhere you need a bold, quick screen. Native to the United States.

SITING AND CARE: Plant in full sun with moderate moisture and good drainage. Let these plants escape the vegetable garden! They are easily grown from seed during warm weather. Borers and other insects occasionally are a problem. Grow these vines on strings, trellises, or chain link fences; let them trail on the ground amidst other plants or over compost or rock piles. They are vigorous but easily controlled by pinching or pruning.

DECUMARIA BARBARA

Wood vamp

- Showy flowers and rich green leaves
- Deciduous to semi evergreen; climbs by rootlets
- Ultimately reaching about 30 feet, grows up to 5 to 8 feet per summer
- Zones 7 to 9

USES: Wood vamp flowers resemble the better-known climbing hydrangea, but this vine is slower growing. The flowers are creamy white and open under rich green foliage in late spring on this generally healthy plant. Its leaves stay green into the winter, browning before spring. Native to southeastern United States.

SITING AND CARE: Plant wood vamp in partial to heavy shade with moderate moisture. This plant can grow to be quite large over time. Careful pruning will help control it.

Wood vamp is a southern native with shiny, dark green leaves and white flowers.

DICENTRA SCANDENS

Climbing bleeding heart

- Yellow flowers all summer long
- Herbaceous; climbs with tendrils
- Grows about 6 to 8 feet per summer
- Zones 7 to 9; can be grown as an annual

USES: One of the finest-textured vines, dicentra has small yellow flowers blooming all summer and well into autumn. They are never terribly showy but are quite pleasant the entire blooming season. The leaves are bluish green in color and quite small. Dicentra is generally healthy. Native to the Himalayas.

SITING AND CARE: Dicentra grows best in light shade with adequate moisture, and is suitable for a trellis, arbor, or on shrubs and small trees. It grows very quickly, and is an excellent choice for containers.

Climbing bleeding heart on a dogwood

DOLICHOS LABLAB

Hyacinth bean

- Purple pods and purple-tinged flowers and leaves
- Climbs by twining
- Grows 12 to 20 feet in a summer
- Zones 9 to 10; usually grown as an annual

USES: This very satisfying annual vine has showy, fragrant flowers, but it is positively stellar when its fat, wide pods start turning purple in mid-summer. Leaves are flushed purple, three leaflets to a purple stalk. It complements silvery conifers or contrasts with bright yellow and orange flowers. It doesn't get thick enough to shade out other plants, so try it on a blue spruce or juniper. Native to tropical Africa.

SITING AND CARE: Plant in full sun with moderate moisture. Grow it on lattice, strings, netting, or a chain link fence. Share the seeds, and your friends will be able to grow hyacinth bean the following summer.

RECOMMENDED CULTIVARS: The nomenclature of this plant is under study, so you may see it called *Lablab purpureus*. 'Ruby Moon' has especially purple pods, and another selection, 'Alba', has pale lavender or white flowers, green leaves, and pods.

The purple pods of hyacinth bean on a lattice

The tubular flowers of 'Tesco Red' glory flower

ECCREMOCARPUS SCABER
Glory flower

- Bold orange and red flowers throughout the summer
- Evergreen, south; annual, north; climbs by tendrils
- Vigorous; grows 10 to 12 feet in a summer
- Zones 9 to 10; roots may overwinter in Zone 8

USES: This is one of the best vines for showy blooms over a long period. Usually grown as an annual, it blooms the first summer from seed. Flowers are tubular and in the "hot" color range (red, yellow, or orange). The leaves are lacy. Use it with other hot colors. Native to Chile.

SITING AND CARE: Plant glory flower in full sun or partial shade with moderate moisture and good drainage. It does well on arbors, trellises, strings, netting, or scrambling over other plants.

RECOMMENDED CULTIVARS: Selections include 'Aureus' with golden yellow flowers, 'Carmineus' with red flowers, and 'Roseus', with pink flowers. 'Tresco Mix' seed produces a mixture of plants with various colored flowers. 'Anglia Hybrids' is a mix of colors, including red, pink, orange, and yellow.

Albo Marginata Wintercreeper

EUONYMUS FORTUNEI
Wintercreeper

- Showy orange fruits
- Evergreen (one of the hardiest); climbs by rootlets
- Generally slow growing, but vigor varies with cultivar
- Zones 5 to 9 (some cultivars hardy to Zone 4)

USES: This cousin of bittersweet is a useful evergreen in northern regions. Some plants produce showy, bittersweet-like orange fruits, which are poisonous. Native to eastern Asia.

SITING AND CARE: Wintercreeper can be grown in full sun or shade with moderate moisture. Where winters are particularly cold, give it protection from winter wind and sun (try it against a southeast-facing wall). These grow best on masonry or tree trunks.

RECOMMENDED CULTIVARS: A wide range of cultivars gives you a choice of leaf colors, showy fruit, and growth habits (vine, shrubby, or ground cover). 'Coloratus' is a vine or ground cover that turns purple in the winter and is one of the hardiest (to zone 4). 'Emerald Gaiety' and 'Albo Marginatus' have white variegated leaves; 'Emerald 'n Gold' and 'Aureo Marginatus', yellow variegation. 'Longwood' and 'Minimus' (also called 'Kewensis') have very small, dark green leaves. 'Vegetus' has bold leaves and produces ample quantities of attractive light orange fruit (hardy to zone 4).

Aureo Marginatus Wintercreeper

FICUS PUMILA

Creeping fig

- Small, neat, dark green leaves
- Evergreen; climbs by rootlets
- Vigorous; grows 10 feet per year
- Zones 8 to 10

USES: This relative of the edible fig is popular in the South outdoors, and as a conservatory plant in the North, for its small, dark, evergreen leaves that cling very closely to the surface they climb on. Older plants sometimes produce fruit (inedible) on horizontal stems that bear larger leaves. Native to eastern Asia.

SITING AND CARE: This plant prefers partial shade and moderate moisture. It is best to trim off horizontal shoots, since neither the larger leaves nor the fruits are desirable.

RECOMMENDED CULTIVARS: 'Minima' is a less vigorous selection with smaller leaves.

With some shearing, creeping fig forms a tight mass on a brick wall.

GELSEMIUM SEMPERVIRENS

Carolina jessamine

- Stellar evergreen with fragrant yellow flowers in early spring
- Climbs by twining
- Vigorous; about 10 to 15 feet per year
- Zones 8 to 10

USES: Beloved in the South, this twining, blooming evergreen is beautiful, but all parts of the plant are poisonous. The showy, trumpetlike, fragrant yellow flowers appear in masses throughout the spring. The foliage tends to be sparse and occasional pruning will help the plant look fuller. The stems are cinnamon brown in color. Native to southeastern United States and Central America.

SITING AND CARE: This vine grows in sun or shade with moderate moisture. Plant on chain link fence, lattice or posts. It is little troubleed by insects.

RECOMMENDED CULTIVARS AND RELATED SPECIES: 'Pride of Augusta' ('Plena') has double flowers, which are showy longer than those of the species. *Gelsemium rankinii* is a nearly identical species, with flowers that are not fragrant.

Jessamine (above and at left) blooms profusely in the spring.

English ivy climbs on almost anything.

'Midas Touch' English ivy with other ivies.

'Gloire de Marengo' Algerian ivy

HEDERA HELIX

English ivy

- Bold, evergreen leaves on a vigorous vine or ground cover
- Climbs with rootlets
- Zones 6 to 10 (zone 5 for a few cultivars)

USES: This is the "true" ivy, with shiny, evergreen leaves. A vigorous grower, it serves equally well as a ground cover or a vine.

Leaves of two types are produced. Standard foliage has five-lobed leaves on easily rooting stems. Such growth is called "juvenile," because seedlings produce this type of foliage. Ivy can stay in this juvenile stage for decades, never flowering or fruiting.

Old plants may eventually produce "mature" foliage, which is diamond-shaped and held horizontally from the main stems. Mature growth produces white clusters of flowers followed by blue-black (sometimes yellowish) fruit. Birds eat the fruit and spread the weedy seedlings.

The evergreen growth complements the straight trunk of trees such as tulip poplars. Birds flock to such protected areas for winter shelter and spring nesting.

Mix other vines with English ivy. Let ivy climb a tree and then plant a clematis to cling to the ivy if there is enough light. You'll have an evergreen background all winter, and the showy clematis flowers will reward you in the summer. Ivy will grow as a ground cover wherever it has a chance. Interplant with bulbs such as daffodils and snowdrops to relieve the monotony of green. The dark ivy leaves set off bright yellow and white strikingly. and hide dying bulb foliage. Native to Eurasia and northern Africa.

SITING AND CARE: English ivy grows in sun or shade and tolerates drought. It roots easily wherever the stems touch the ground. Propagation is done simply by cutting shoots with preformed roots and planting the shoots directly where new plants are wanted. Mulch soil around cuttings and don't let them dry out. New leaves will develop, indicating the plant is becoming established. Spring is the best time to take cuttings, before new growth starts, but it is possible throughout the summer and early fall. The milder the winter, the stronger this plant's vigor. Ivy is a staple of most southern gardens and is often cursed for being too vigorous. In the North, greater care is needed for successful planting. In the northern regions of zone 6 (and in zone 5), protect ivy from winter wind and sun. Otherwise, the leaves will "burn" (they will regrow). There are few structures it is unable to conquer (it will even grow on aluminum siding and glass blocks), but it's ideal on masonry, trees, or (with a little help) on lattice and chain link. Regular pruning is needed on buildings to keep the new growth from invading windows and doors and from growing under siding and shingles.

RECOMMENDED CULTIVARS: In northern gardens, use only the hardiest cultivars. Use the special leaf sizes and shapes where they will be noticed and add to the textural display. Yellow and white variegated ivies brighten dark spots. Any of the cultivars may "revert" or mutate back to standard green leaves. If a change in growth occurs, cut it off before it overtakes the original plant.

'Baltica', 'Bulgaria', 'Ogallala', 'Romania', and 'Thorndale' are the most cold hardy selections. Use them for planting in zone 5. 'Star' has five very pointed lobes and serves equally well as a ground cover and a vine; leaves are 2 inches long.

'Tomboy' has triangular leaves with rounded edges. It readily climbs and often blooms and produces fruit.

'Gold Craft' leaves are small (1 to 1½ inches) and golden, but tend to brown in the winter. 'Gold Child' is not vigorous and doesn't climb well.

Algerian ivy, *Hedera canariensis* (also called *H. algeriensis*), has large (to 6 inches), smooth, evergreen leaves and is useful in zone 9 (zone 8 with protection) southward. It, too, forms a ground cover and climbs with rootlets. Persian ivy, *Hedera colchica*, is similar to Algerian ivy, but hardier (zone 7). It produces bolder leaves than English ivy.

'Anne Marie'

'Gold Heart'

'Cavendishii'

'Gold Nugget'

'Luzii'

'Glacier'

'Bulgaria'

'Gold Child'

'White Knight'

'Ivalace'

'Deltoidea'

'Chrysophylla'

'Buttercup'

'Gold Heart'

'Glacier'

'Bruder Ingobert'

Use golden hop (Humulus lupulus 'Aureus') to brighten dark-colored walls.

HUMULUS LUPULUS

European hop

- Bright foliage, fragrant flowers
- Herbaceous, climbs by twining
- Grows 10 to 15 feet in a season
- Zone 5 to 8

USES: This is the hop used to flavor beer but is grown in gardens for its foliage. The fragrant, straw-colored female flowers resemble small bags and appear in late summer. They are followed by similar-looking fruits, which can be dried for use in arrangements. Native to Europe and North America.

SITING AND CARE: In the garden, this vine is valuable for its quick foliage effect.

The fruit (from female plants only) is considered an additional interest. The leaves resemble deeply lobed maple leaves and are covered with fine hairs, which can irritate bare skin.

Hops will grow in sun or shade, but foliage has more vivid color in full sun. Tolerant of drought, hops need good drainage. Plant them on posts, trellises, and wires, or let them scramble over other plants. Hops will look neater if you remove the old stems before new growth starts in the spring. Aphids are an occasional problem.

RECOMMENDED CULTIVARS: The cultivar 'Aureus' has golden yellow leaves and is the most commonly grown hop for the garden. It needs strong light to develop its color. The golden leaves are especially effective against a dark green or purple background. Japanese hop, *Humulus japonicus*, has leaves with five to seven lobes (compared to three to five on European hop). Its leaves and stems are very rough to the touch and can irritate skin upon contact. It is a noxious weed in some areas. Some gardeners like it, however, for its colored foliage cultivars. 'Lutescens' has lime green leaves; 'Variegatus' leaves are streaked and blotched with white.

Climbing hydrangea has showy white spring flowers and yellow autumn color.

Climbing hydrangea in early summer (top) and autumn.

HYDRANGEA PETIOLARIS

Climbing hydrangea

- Creamy white flowers in late spring
- Deciduous; climbs by rootlets
- Slow to moderate growth rate
- Zones 5 to 7

USES: Creamy white flowers appear in late spring against a background of deep green, shiny leaves. The flower clusters are lacy (sometimes described as "lace cap"), with large, four-sepaled blossoms surrounding a center mass of small flowers lacking petals. They appear on 1- to 2-foot-long horizontal shoots. The clusters dry to an attractive tan. Remaining until the following spring, they are especially pleasant in the winter when dusted with snow. In autumn, the leaves often turn bright yellow before falling. During the winter months, the peeling bark provides interest.

Be patient with climbing hydrangea. Even if you purchase a blooming plant, the vine may put all its energy into leafy growth and you may have to wait up to five years to see flowers. The wait is worth it, and the display will generously increase every year.

Combine climbing hydrangea with English ivy to achieve an evergreen effect. The ivy will grow underneath the hydrangea, providing a perfect backdrop for the white hydrangea flowers. Climbing hydrangea can also be grown as a large shrub. Plant away from structures, and let it pile on top of itself. Native to eastern Asia.

SITING AND CARE: Although it can grow in full sun, it thrives with at least a bit of shade. It requires average moisture and good drainage. To propagate by cuttings, in early spring, remove 6-inch-long shoots with rootlets present. Bury the bottom two-thirds of the stem. New growth should start by late May. Japanese beetles can skeletonize the leaves, especially those in full sun. Shaded leaves seem of less interest to these pests.

Little pruning is needed with climbing hydrangea, but prune it away from windows. This is an excellent choice for substantial masonry walls and the trunks of mature trees. It will clothe a wall with white flowers, and turn a dull trunk into a floral masterpiece.

RECOMMENDED CULTIVARS: 'Brookside Littleleaf' has small (1½ to 2 inches) leaves and is especially attractive trailing out of a container.

Moonflower

■ Large, night-blooming, fragrant white flowers
■ Climbs by twining
■ Grows 10 feet or more per summer
■ Usually grown as an annual, except in Zones 8 to 10

USES: Big, bold, and magical—all describe this nocturnal wonder. Six-inch-wide fragrant flowers start opening in late afternoon, unfurling as you watch. They stay open during the evening (attracting desirable nocturnal moths) but are only a memory when morning arrives. The dark green leaves reach 9 inches in width and are a show in themselves. Moonflower's nativity is not known; it seems to be native throughout the tropics.

SITING AND CARE: Plant moonflowers in full sun with average moisture. Moonflower is easily grown from seed. Nick the seeds with a file or knife and soak them overnight before planting. This nicking (called scarification) speeds germination. Start seeds inside about four weeks before the expected last frost. Alternatively plant directly outside after all danger of frost has passed. Moonflowers grow slowly until hot weather hits, and then they reach for the stars!

Plant moonflowers near patios and walkways where you will notice them each summer evening. Grow them on netting, a trellis, or a chain link fence. Construct a ladder of bamboo poles and let the moonflowers ascend.

Moonflowers open so quickly that you can watch them in early evening. On cloudy days, they will often stay open into the morning.

Sweet potato vine

■ Colorful foliage all summer
■ Sprawls on other plants or on the ground
■ Grows at least 10 feet per summer
■ Zones 9 to 10; or as an annual

USES: This is the species you buy as sweet potatoes in the store. Easily grown in areas with hot summers, the species is usually included in the garden as only a food plant (albeit an attractive one). The ornamental cultivars produce edible (but not tasty) underground tubers by the end of the summer. You can dig and store these tubers in a dark, cool place during the winter, and replant them the next spring. Native to eastern Asia.

SITING AND CARE: After the danger of frost has passed, plant the tubers an inch under the soil in full sun or light shade and provide moderate moisture. For extra plants during the growing season, cut off 6-inch stems and place in a glass of water. They will root and can be planted in the garden.

Insects may attack the plants in midsummer, damaging the foliage. If they do, cut back the stems to a foot or two.

Undamaged new growth will soon cover the plants. Rabbits, too, enjoy the foliage. If they are a problem, plant your vine in a container above the reach of bunnies.

RECOMMENDED CULTIVARS: Sweet potato vine cultivars offer excellent foliage color all summer long. 'Blackie' has deep purple (almost black) foliage, which is fantastic trailing out of a terra-cotta pot or amidst other plants. It contrasts beautifully with yellow, chartreuse, and silver leaves and flowers. 'Margarita' has chartreuse foliage and illuminates dark-leaved plants and flowers. It is even stunning just against dark brown mulch. 'Tricolor' has pink, white, and green variegation, but lacks vigor.

Top and bottom, 'Blackie' sweet potato. Center: 'Margarita'.

Cardinal climber is a hybrid of cypress vine and scarlet starglory.

Cardinal climber

- Bright red flowers are produced throughout the summer
- Annual; climbs by twining
- Grows about 10 feet a summer

USES: *Ipomoea × sloteri* (also known as *I. × multifida*), the cardinal climber, has bright red blossoms with bright yellow centers, and deeply lobed leaves, coarser than those of cypress vine (see below). The bright green leaves are the perfect backdrop for the showy, scarlet flowers. The flowers open in the morning, close later in the day, and attract hummingbirds.

SITING AND CARE: Cardinal climber grows best in full sun with average moisture. Plant seeds directly where you want the plants, after all danger of frost is past. For more rapid germination, nick the hard seed coat with a file and soak the seed overnight before sowing.

The vine is great on netting, a chain link fence, small lattices, and in containers. Try it near a walkway you use in the morning to start the day off on a bright note.

Cypress vine has extremely fine-textured, cut leaves. The tubular, star-shaped flowers are normally red, but white strains can be found.

Cypress vine

- Scarlet flowers and lacy, cut leaves
- Annual; climbs by twining
- Grows 10 to 20 feet a summer

USES: These showy, scarlet flowers are the shape of five-pointed stars and are held above deeply cut, feathery leaves.
Although flowers are small, they are produced in showy masses. Occasionally white and red flowers can appear on the same plant.
Contrast the fine texture of the leaves with something big and bold, such as Dutchman's pipe or an oakleaf hydrangea. Native to tropical America.

SITING AND CARE: Cypress vine thrives in full sun. It needs average moisture with good drainage. Grow from seed. Nick the hard seed coat with a file and soak the seed overnight before sowing. Have it climb trellises, bamboo poles, netting, and chain link fences. It's a great subject for containers, too.

IPOMOEA TRICOLOR

Morning glory

- Fast-growing with showy flowers
- Annual
- Grows 10 feet or more a summer

USES: This vine is a performer. It grows once hot weather arrives and rewards you with beautiful, funnel-shaped, 3-inch-wide flowers from mid to late summer until the first frost.

Flowers open in the morning, then fade and drop in the afternoon, although they may stay open on cloudy days or on cool autumn days. Leaves are deep green, heart-shaped, and about 3 to 4 inches long. Morning glory is occasionally bothered by rust or mildew. It may self-seed and become weedy, especially in the South. Seeds are poisonous if eaten. Native to Mexico and Central America.

SITING AND CARE: Morning glories grow in sun or partial shade in soil with average moisture and good drainage. Grow from seed by nicking the hard seed coat with a file and soaking the seed overnight before sowing. Soils with low fertility are best; rich soil favors more foliage than flowers.

Grow morning glories on strings, netting, or chain link fences, let them scramble over other plants, or try them in containers.

RECOMMENDED CULTIVARS: Combine the sky-blue, white-throated flowers of the cultivar 'Heavenly Blue' with grays and other blues. 'Pearly Gates' is a pure white with a yellow throat and will brighten a dark area. 'Blue Star' has light blue flowers with darker blue stripes radiating from the center. 'Early Call' has large flowers that are a mix of cerise and blue, white in the center and on the edges. 'Scarlet Star' blossoms are red with a white edge and white, with a star-shaped center.

Two other species (*Ipomoea nil* and *I. purpurea*) plus many hybrids are very similar and are also sold under the name of morning glory. *I. nil* is called the Japanese morning glory, and its cultivar 'Scarlett O'Hara' has large rose-red flowers with leaves blotched with white. *I. purpurea* selections include the white-flowered 'Alba', white and red 'Madame Anne', and the double-flowered purple 'Violacea'.

Morning glories grow vigorously once warm weather arrives. The flowers open in the cool of the morning and close by the hot afternoon.

A sampling of the colors available with morning glories.

Pink Chinese jasmine covers itself with blush pink, fragrant flowers for most of the growing season.

JASMINUM POLYANTHUM

Pink Chinese jasmine

■ Showy, fragrant pink flowers bloom over a long period. Finely cut, narrow, dark green leaves
■ Deciduous to evergreen; grows by scrambling and twining
■ Grows up to 15 feet tall
■ Zones 9 to 10; also used in conservatories

USES: The very showy flowers (up to ¾ inch wide) are produced over a long period of time, from late spring into autumn. It is very attractive against blues, grays, and blacks. Native to China.

SITING AND CARE: Give the plant full sun and protection from the wind in colder areas. It is vigorous, tolerant of drought, and needs good drainage.

Weave the stems into lattice or let it twine around supports. Train it up a south-facing wall or over an arch where you will appreciate the fragrance.

RELATED SPECIES: Winter-flowering jasmine, *Jasminum nudiflorum*, is another Chinese species. Its yellow, unscented flowers appear sporadically throughout the winter and are set off against green stems. This plant is especially attractive cascading from a container or when trained upright and allowed to cascade down itself. Plant it with weeping forsythia to extend the effective bloom period. It is hardy in zones 6 to 9. It cannot climb by itself and needs to be tied or woven in to a support.

The long green stems of Jasminum nudiflorum are easily trained upward onto a fence then cascade downward.

Interesting and exotically different, hanging gourds bring out the child in everyone.

LAGENARIA SICERARIA

Bottle gourd

■ Fascinatingly large and useful fruits
■ Annual; climbs by tendrils
■ Very vigorous; grows 20 to 30 feet in a summer

USES: Imagine walking through an arbor, dodging two-foot-long hanging gourds. This magical experience is yours for the planting. Imagine how kids will react! If you don't have an arbor, train the vine onto a small tree, or on a chain link fence. Leaves are large (to 10 inches), soft, medium green, and hairy. Flowers are 2 to 3 inches and white (occasionally yellow) in color. Seed mixtures are often available, giving you a variety of gourd shapes, including dipper, club, bottle, dumbbell, powder horn, kettle, and trough. These are whimsical plants and the seeds are inexpensive. The harvested gourds can be used as ornaments, drilled and hung as bird houses, or cut open to use as dippers. The uses are limited only by your imagination, and the gourds will last for a year or two. Remember to save some seeds to use in future plantings. Native throughout the tropics.

SITING AND CARE: Grow in full sun and give them moderate moisture. Like squash or pumpkins, they require a long, hot growing season. Directly sow in the garden after all danger of frost has passed, or start seeds indoors about a month before the frost-free date. The farther north you are, the greater the need for starting indoors. The plants need four frost-free months to develop the gourds. Give them plenty of room because these are vigorous growers. Whiteflies, borers and mildew are occasionally problems.

LATHYRUS ODORATUS

Annual sweet pea

■ Showy, fragrant flowers
■ Annual; excellent for areas with cool summers; grows by tendrils
■ Grows to about 6 feet

USES: This flowering vine inspires "oohs" and "aahs" from sentimentalists who remember the pretty flowers and sweet fragrance from a parent's or grandparent's garden. Flower colors vary from white to rose, red, and violet. Fragrance also varies from plant to plant, although purples seem to be more consistently fragrant. Native to Crete and Italy.

SITING AND CARE: Annual sweet peas grow best in cool climates. They tolerate some frost and should be planted in early spring, as early as the ground can be worked. To speed germination, soak the seeds for a day or two before planting. Plant them in the sun in moderately moist soil with good drainage. Flowers will cease if you let the hairy inedible fruit pods develop. Sweet pea does poorly in hot summers. Gardens in northern regions and near cool bodies of water are perfect, and flowers may continue all summer long.

Grow sweet peas on netting, strings, or lattice, amidst summer-blooming shrubs, or in containers.

RELATED SPECIES: Everlasting pea (*Lathyrus grandiflorus*) and perennial pea (*L. latifolius*) are herbaceous perennials, rather than annuals. They die to the ground each autumn, resprouting the following spring. Both climb with tendrils and bloom in early summer. Everlasting pea grows to be about 6 feet tall and has mildly fragrant, pinkish purple flowers. Perennial pea grows to nine feet and is vigorous enough to become weedy in gardens.

These perennial sweet peas are sold as seeds or as plants. Grow them on trellises, lattices, chain link fences, or netting. Watch out with perennial pea. It may take over an area and is best planted by itself, perhaps to cover a sloping site or rock pile.

Sweet peas add fragrance and a relaxed, old-fashioned look to a garden. Keep them well watered to encourage bloom.

'Old Spice'

'Souvenir'

'Mrs. Joan Ward'

'Remembrance'

'Oban Bay'

'Mars'

LONICERA SEMPERVIRENS

Trumpet honeysuckle

■ **Attractive flowers from spring until fall**
■ **Deciduous; climbs by twining**
■ **Slow to moderate growth rate, eventually reaching 10 to 15 feet**
■ **Zones 4 to 9**

USES: This vine has the longest blooming season of any of the hardy climbers. Flowers open in midspring and continue putting on a show until they succumb to heavy frosts in autumn. Individual flowers are tubular and borne in showy clusters. They are not fragrant but hummingbirds enjoy them. The flowers are followed by clusters of berries that are relished by other birds. The leaves are bluish green, and the terminal leaf pairs tend to fuse together into one. Native to United States.

SITING AND CARE: This vine tolerates shade but blooms best in the sun. It needs average moisture; avoid drought for best results.

Plant a honeysuckle on an arch or an arbor, with a small shrub or a perennial at the base to hide the stems. Honeysuckle will also climb trellises, lattice, netting, chain link fences, bamboo tripods, or even a single strand of rope. Place it where you will be able to observe the hummingbirds at a short distance without frightening them. Aphids are a major nuisance. The aphids attack heavily in the spring, and the plant may outgrow them without sprays by early summer. Spraying one or two times with horticultural oil or an insecticide is effective.

RECOMMENDED CULTIVARS AND RELATED SPECIES: There are a number of selections of trumpet honeysuckle to choose for gardens.

Lonicera sempervirens 'Sulphurea' and 'John Clayton' have yellow flowers. 'John Clayton' is a newer selection and seems to be more floriferous and attractive than 'Sulphurea'. 'Magnifica' and 'Superba' have scarlet flowers;

Trumpet honeysuckle 'Superba' has tubular flowers that are redder than those generally found on this species.

'Cedar Lane' has long (to 2 inches), dark red flowers.

Besides trumpet honeysuckle, there are a number of related species and cultivars that are outstanding for gardens.

Lonicera × *brownii*, scarlet trumpet honeysuckle, is primarily known for the selection 'Dropmore Scarlet'. It produces large numbers of orange-red flowers throughout the summer and is hardy to zone 3. Lonicera 'Mandarin' has long (2 to 3 inches) reddish orange flowers on vigorously growing plants.

Yellow honeysuckle (*Lonicera flava*) is native to the Southeast and has apricot-to-orange-colored flowers and rounded, bluish green leaves. The terminal leaves are fused, cupping beneath the flowers. The flower color is perfect with the purples of some clematis cultivars, especially selections of *Clematis viticella*. Yellow honeysuckle blooms in late spring to early summer, followed by red berries late in the summer. Hardy to zones 6 to 9, it grows at a moderate rate to about 12 feet tall.

Lonicera × *heckrottii*, goldflame honeysuckle, has a long bloom season with showy maroon flowers, opening wide to display a yellow interior. Hardy in most of zones 4 to 9, it grows much like trumpet honeysuckle, but offers fragrant blooms from late spring through summer. Unfortunately, it does not attract hummingbirds.

Woodbine is the name given to several vines, including *Lonicera periclymenum*. This European honeysuckle is hardy to zones 5 to 9 and is vigorous, growing to about 20 feet. Its scented flowers open ivory colored with a purple exterior and appear sporadically throughout the summer months. Clusters of dark red berries follow the flowers. Aphids will attack it but never seem to be as much of a problem as they are with trumpet honeysuckle.

'Serotina' is one of the more commonly available cultivars. Its leaves have a distinctly purplish cast to them. Its flowers are yellow on the inside, deep purple outside. 'Aurea' has yellow variegated leaves. Berries Jubilee™ ('Monul') has yellow flowers; 'Graham Thomas' provides white to yellow flowers lacking purple.

The evergreen Giant Burmese honeysuckle, *L. hildebrandiana*, is a, showy, vigorous honeysuckle for warm climates (zone 10 southward). It bears clusters of huge, fragrant, creamy yellow flowers early in the summer.

Etruscan honeysuckle, *L. etrusca*, and its cultivar 'Superba', are showier than trumpet honeysuckle and are very floriferous, with creamy white to orange flowers. It is hardy in zones 7 (perhaps 6) to 9.

Goldflame honeysuckle is a hybrid of trumpet honeysuckle with bicolor flowers and a long bloom season.

Lonicera × tellmanniana is another trumpet honeysuckle hybrid with rich orange flowers all summer.

Lonicera × brownii 'Dropmore Scarlet' bears deep orange-red flowers throughout summer.

Yellow flowers and red berries of Lonicera periclymenum 'Monul' (Berries Jubilee™)

The two-toned flowers of Lonicera periclymenum 'Serotina' are showy and fragrant.

The 6-inch, creamy yellow flowers of giant Burmese honeysuckle are almost overpoweringly fragrant.

THE UNWANTED HONEYSUCKLE

One species that should be strictly avoided is Japanese honeysuckle, *Lonicera japonica*. This Asian vine is such a prevalent weed in the eastern and southern United States that many people think it is native to these areas. It blooms in summer in the East and in spring in the South with extremely fragrant, yellow and white flowers, followed by showy black fruit. Summer heat reduces flowering, but it produces more flowers in the fall. It seeds into garden and natural areas and is very difficult to kill. It girdles and shades out native trees and may overrun entire woodlots.

The yellow and white flowers of Japanese honeysuckle can scent an entire area and are followed by shiny black fruit. Unfortunately this vine is a rampant pest.

Vegetable sponge has showy yellow flowers and long green fruit that can be used as bath sponges.

LUFFA CYLINDRICA

Vegetable sponge

- Showy yellow flowers and spongelike fruit
- Annual; climbs by tendrils
- Vigorous; grows to 20 feet

USES: This vine produces a fruit that resembles a cucumber and has similarly large (to 8 inches) and lobed (but not hairy) leaves. Dried and peeled, it can be used as a bath sponge. The flowers are yellow and relatively showy. The vine is probably more fun than aesthetic but is easy to grow. The large leaves are dense and excellent for short-term screening. Prepare the sponges by holding the mature fruit in running water until skin and seeds and pulp are washed away. Then lay them out in the sun for a few weeks until they are dried. Native to tropical Asia and Africa.

SITING AND CARE: Grow this plant in full sun in moderately moist soil with good drainage. The plants grow vigorously once hot weather arrives. Sow the seeds directly or start them indoors a month before the last frost. The plants need a long, hot growing season and will grow vigorously once hot weather arrives. Train luffa onto a strong structure, such as an arbor, a chain link fence, or the lower branches of a tree (the drooping fruit will be fun to walk under).

One way to get it to grow up into a tree is to plant the seed (or seedling) in full sun on the south side of a tree. Using a bamboo pole as a nurse stake, train luffa upwards to the tree limb. Once the vine reaches the tree, it will take care of itself. Whiteflies and borers are occasionally a problem.

The deep pink flowers of Red Riding Hood mandevilla bloom for most of the summer in a hot, sunny spot.

MANDEVILLA X AMABILIS

Mandevilla

- Continuous bloom throughout the summer
- Evergreen; climbs by twining
- Vigorous; grows to 15 feet a season
- Tropical (zone 10); grown as an annual in the North

USES: This tropical performs so well in the northern summer garden that it is worth its price just for one growing season. It is sold as a container plant (as opposed to being available as a seed, like many of the annual vines). The trumpet-shaped, 3- to 4-inch-wide flowers open pale pink and deepen to a rosy red, and are a complement near pink or purple foliage and flowers. Leaves are shiny, dark green, and up to 8 inches long. It is generally pest-free when grown outdoors.

SITING AND CARE: Grow mandevilla in a container in full sun or light shade and keep the soil moderately moist. Feature it on a sunny patio. Prune back any wayward long shoots or weave them into the lattice, chain link, or trellis on which the plant is growing. Fertilize every two or three weeks, keep it watered, and it will bloom the entire summer and well into autumn.

Let mandevilla die with frost or bring it indoors for the winter. (Don't expect a good display during the winter; it most likely will go dormant and lose many of its leaves.) If you overwinter it, cut it back hard in the spring for strong new growth and flowers.

RECOMMENDED CULTIVARS: The cultivar 'Alice du Pont' has rosy pink flowers with a darker throat. 'Peter Pan' has red flowers. Janell™ is an especially heavy bloomer with rose red flowers, and its close sister Leah™ is blush pink.

The closely related *Mandevilla sanderi* 'Red Riding Hood' has deep pink flowers with a yellow center. It is less vigorous, only growing 6 to 8 feet a season. Another relative, known as Chilean jasmine (*M. laxa*) has fragrant white flowers.

MINA LOBATA

Spanish flag

■ Long-blooming season of red and yellow flowers
■ Climbs by twining
■ Grows 10 to 20 feet a season
■ Tropical; usually grown as an annual

USES: The erect clusters of this showy vine bear red and yellow flowers that face one direction, as if they were flags blowing in the wind. (The flag of Spain is yellow and red striped, hence the plant's name.) This climber is closely related to morning glories and is sometimes listed in the same genus, as *Ipomoea lobata*, although its flowers do not open wide like morning glories but instead are 1-inch-long tubes. The deeply lobed, dark green leaves do resemble their morning glory cousins, however. Use it to brighten dark areas or plant it with other reds, yellows, and oranges. The colors also go well with dark purples. Native to Mexico.

SITING AND CARE: Spanish flag grows best in full sun. It needs moderately moist soil with good drainage. Mina is easily started from seed in the spring and is generally unbothered by pests. Grow it on fences, trellises, or netting.

RECOMMENDED CULTIVARS: 'Citronella' has cream flowers and red buds. 'Mexican Fiesta' has red and yellow flowers.

The blossoms of Spanish flag stand out from the plant like banners.

MENISPERMUM CANADENSE

Moonseed

■ Handsome dark green leaves
■ Deciduous; climbs by twining
■ Grows 5 to 12 feet a year
■ Zones 5 to 9

USES: This quietly beautiful native vine makes a good foliage screen and background. The leaves are lustrous and dark green, maplelike but with rounded lobes. It grows rapidly once established and makes a very dense screen. It often dies back in the winter but quickly grows back in the spring. Flowers are inconspicuous, and female plants produce clusters of blue-black fruit resembling grapes. This fruit is handsome yet dangerous because it is poisonous. Use moonseed as a background for brightly colored flowers or play up its textural effect by contrasting it with something very finely textured. Native to eastern North America.

SITING AND CARE: Moonseed grows in sun or shade with moderate moisture.

Grow moonseed as a thick cover on chain link fences. It will also climb poles and netting. One drawback is that it suckers profusely. Planting it near a lawn is perfect since the suckers will be cut down by the mower. Next to a flower bed the vine could wreak havoc. It is generally pest free.

Moonseed is grown for its attractive, dark green leaves, which are rarely bothered by pests and display themselves well throughout the summer.

PARTHENOCISSUS TRICUSPIDATA

Boston ivy

■ Deep green leaves and neat habit
■ Deciduous; climbs like a rootlet vine by tendrils tipped with adhesive discs
■ Vigorous once established; grows 6 to 10 feet per year
■ Zones 4 to 8

USES: This, the "ivy" of the Ivy League, covers the buildings of many northeastern United States universities and turns them into green boxes. On the fence at Fenway Park, its color changes with the season: light green in spring, dark green in summer, and scarlet in fall.

This is one of the flattest-growing vines. Its stems grow tight against a structure, with only individual leaves sticking out. The dark green leaves resemble three-pointed maple leaves. Leaf width varies from 4 to 8 inches. Flowers are small, green, and hard to find. They develop into blue-black berries on red stalks, becoming apparent after the leaves fall. Birds consume the berries before winter arrives.

Occasionally young plants and fast-growing shoots form "juvenile" leaves with three leaflets. Autumn color is a screaming peach to scarlet crimson. Fall color is best in full sun, becoming pale yellow in heavy shade. Winter effect is a dense tracery of thin stems.

Boston ivy will tightly adhere to masonry walls, forming a very dark mass of foliage. Use it as a backdrop for summer flowers, especially reds, yellows, oranges, and whites. It differs from other tendril vines in that the tendrils do not clasp. Instead, they have adhesive discs at their tips that cling like

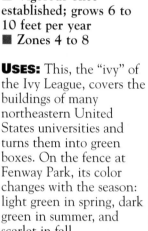

When growing in full sun, the three-pointed leaves of Boston ivy turn a stunning red in autumn.

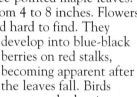

The summer color of Boston ivy

rootlet-type climbers. Native to Eastern Asia.

SITING AND CARE: Boston ivy grows in shade and tolerates drought. Although it will grow in sun, the reflected heat of south-facing masonry walls may inhibit new growth. In such cases, plant the vine on an adjacent east- or west-facing wall and allow it to climb into the sun. It is generally pest-free, although Japanese beetles may damage leaves in sun.

RECOMMENDED CULTIVARS: Cultivars 'Lowii' and 'Veitchii' have small (under 3 inches) leaves. 'Beverley Brook' has leaves half the normal size. All three are significantly less vigorous than the species. 'Green Spring' and 'Green Showers' have glossy leaves up to 10 inches across. 'Purpurea' has reddish-purple leaves; 'Aurata' has yellow foliage marbled with green and red.

Once established, Boston ivy is extremely vigorous and must be trimmed away from doors and windows annually.

Boston ivy clings with tendrils tipped with adhesive discs, which attach themselves securely to flat surfaces.

PARTHENOCISSUS QUINQUEFOLIA

Virginia creeper

■ Trouble-free, vigorous native with great fall color

■ Deciduous; sometimes climbs by tendrils that have adhesive discs

■ Grows 5 to 10 feet per year

■ Zones 3 to 9

USES: Virginia creeper is commonly found in eastern forests, growing as a vine and as a ground cover. It offers bold leaves divided into five leaflets, each 4 to 5 inches long. Dark green during the summer, they turn a brilliant red (in the sun) in autumn. The flowers are inconspicuous, but the waxy, blue-black fruit resembles small Concord grapes and are borne on red stalks. The fruit and stalks complement the autumn leaves and remain showy for several weeks after leaf drop. Birds eat the fruit before winter. Native to eastern North America.

SITING AND CARE: Virginia creeper needs average moisture and grows in sun or shade. This tough climber grows almost anywhere and on almost anything, forming a solid mass of foliage. It wraps its tendrils around structures and plants, and with its adhesive discs at the tips of the tendrils it climbs easily on rocks and masonry. Use it to cover slopes and unsightly areas. It tolerates soil compaction and smog, as well as seaside salt. Most gardeners feel it is too vigorous and not sufficiently showy for key garden areas. However, Virginia creeper is perfect for areas of low maintenance and low visibility. You can easily prune it to control overly vigorous growth. Simply cut unwanted shoots just above a leaf or a bud. The only pest problem is Japanese beetles, and these tend only to attack plants growing in the sun.

RECOMMENDED CULTIVARS: The cultivar 'Engelmannii' (Engelmann ivy) has smaller leaflets (4 inches) than the species but otherwise is very similar.

Silvervein creeper (*Parthenocissus henryana*), is also similar to Virginia creeper, but is less vigorous and has more attractively colored leaves. The leaflets are less than 4 inches long, reddish as they open in the spring, and dark green with silvery veins in the summer. The undersides are purplish red. Fall color is deep red.

Use this Chinese native as an accent plant. It won't overwhelm an area and the leaves are beautiful up close. Instead of forming a dense mass, this plant is open in appearance and lacy in effect. Use it with granite, other pink stones, or anything pink or rust-colored. Grow it in partial shade; it is fully hardy from the southern part of zones 6 to 9.

Virginia creeper, here growing with evergreen English ivy, turns scarlet in autumn.

True to its name, silvervein creeper (left, and right) has distinctly light-colored veins. Whenever the vine is grown in the sun, its leaves turn red in fall.

The five-parted, green leaves of Virginia creeper during the summer

PASSIFLORA CAERULEA

Blue passionflower

■ Showy, fascinating flowers
■ Semievergreen to evergreen; climbs by tendrils
■ Grows 10 to 15 feet per year
■ Zones 8 to 10, or grown as an annual

Passionflowers have unique, fascinating flowers. In the North, use them as summer annuals for a tropical effect.

USES: The radially blue-and-white-centered symmetrical blossoms of blue passionflower are legendary and bloom throughout the summer. The fruits, which are rarely produced, are about 2 inches long, edible and tasty. The leaves are medium green in color, with five lobes. Plant cup-and-saucer vine (*Cobaea*) nearby to repeat the two-tone effect. In any location, cut overly long shoots or weave them among the other stems.

The plant dies to the ground in cold winters (zone 8) but grows back vigorously from the roots. North of zone 8, winter kills the plant. Native to southern Brazil and Argentina.

SITING AND CARE: Grow this vine in full sun or light shade in well-drained, moist soil. Have it climb on lattice or netting near a path. Grow it in a large pot on a patio or try it on an obelisk used as a focal point against a dark background. It is generally pest free.

RECOMMENDED CULTIVARS: 'Grandiflora' has larger flowers (to 6 inches across, compared to 4 inches on the species); 'Constance Elliott' has white flowers.

Maypop (*Passiflora incarnata*) is native to the southeastern United States. The flowers are pinkish white with purple markings, blooming from midsummer into autumn. They are followed by edible yellow, apricot-size fruits. Use maypop as a ground cover, allowing it to scramble over shrubs. Let it climb on a trellis and combine it with other white flowers. It is hardy in zones 7 to 10.

Yellow passionflower (*P. lutea*) is the hardiest of the genus. It is native to the Southeast and grows northward to the southern part of zone 6 to 9. Unfortunately, the greenish yellow flowers are less than an inch across and not very showy.

Red passionflower (*P. coccinea*) is a tropical, with hot red flowers up to 5 inches across. Use it as a potted summer annual in a hot, sunny spot.

PHASEOLUS COCCINEUS

Scarlet runner bean

■ Quick cover and attractive flowers
■ Grows to 15 feet
■ Annual; climbs by twining

Scarlet runner beans cover and hide this chain link fence.

A close-up of the brilliant flowers of scarlet runner bean

USES: Combine your aesthetic and culinary desires with this red-flowered, edible bean. Flowers start by midsummer and continue until frost, especially if the broad, flat pods are kept picked. The scarlet flowers contrast nicely against the vine's green leaves. The plants are especially attractive on olive green lattice or when combined with blue flowers. Plant them with Virginia creeper to add summer color to a planting.

SITING AND CARE: Grow scarlet runner beans in the sun in soil with average moisture and good drainage. Let the vine climb on strings, poles, netting, chain link fences, or lattice. Grow this as you would any pole bean—plant the seeds in a warm, sunny spot after all danger of frost has passed. The flat pods are tasty if eaten while very small. Old pods produce edible shell beans (these can also be used to produce next year's crop). Extra water during times of drought encourages flowering. Native to tropical America.

RECOMMENDED CULTIVARS: 'Albus' and 'The Czar' have white flowers; 'Painted Lady', has a mixture of salmon and white flowers; 'Sunset' blossoms are salmon. 'Purple Aztec' has bright orange-red flowers against purple-flushed stems and leaves.

POLYGONUM AUBERTII

Silver lace vine

■ A cascade of white flowers in late summer
■ Deciduous; climbs by twining
■ Grows to 10 to 20 feet a summer
■ Zones 4 to 8

USES: This vine brings bright white flowers to tired late-summer gardens. The individual flowers are small but borne in a profusion of lacy clusters. The thin, arrowhead-shaped leaves have a fine texture and are small (under 4 inches long). Native to western China.

SITING AND CARE: Grow this plant in sun or light shade. Give it average moisture; it tolerates drought. It blooms on new wood and can be cut back hard in the spring.

Silver lace vine will quickly cover a chain link fence, netting, and shrubs. Try it on a yew hedge, which the climber will brighten with a fluffy coat of white. It is quite vigorous, so cut it to the ground every other year to keep it from overwhelming the yew. Occasionally Japanese beetles will attack foliage.

Silver lace vine covers itself in white flowers in late summer. Blooming on new wood, the vigorous vine can be cut back hard each winter to control its growth.

RHODOCHITON ATROSANGUINEUS

Purple bell vine

■ Showy, purplish-pink flowers from midsummer on
■ Climbs by twining and a clasping leafstalk
■ Grows to 10 feet
■ Tropical perennial treated as an annual

USES: The small flowers look like pink bells with purple clappers. They remain showy for several weeks, and new blooms are produced all summer long. They are especially attractive when viewed from below. Try purple bell vine on arches or even in hanging baskets. Its purple is great with yellows and oranges, as well as with silvery blue conifers. Train it to grow over the top of a dwarf blue spruce. Native to Mexico.

SITING AND CARE: Grow purple bell vine in a sunny spot and give it moderate moisture. Start seeds indoors about six to eight weeks before the last frost or sow the seeds directly after all danger of frost has passed.

Grow it on strings, chain link fences, trellises, or on other plants. It is generally pest free.

The two-tone flowers of purple bell vine look like miniature maroon bells with purple clappers.

ROSA

Climbing and rambling roses

■ **Stunning flowers**
■ **Deciduous; scramblers need to be tied to supports**
■ **Size varies with species and cultivar**
■ **Many are hybrids**
■ **Zones vary with species and cultivar**

USES: Grow these plants for their exuberant masses of flowers. They are excellent cut flowers, and one shoot alone can produce a bouquet.

These roses are actually shrubs with extremely long shoots. They have no mechanism other than thorns for climbing and need to be tied to structures. Roses with extra-long stems are divided into two major divisions: ramblers and climbers.

Climbers generally produce large-size flowers, have stiff, thick stems, and are less vigorous than ramblers. Many will bloom heavily in early summer and then continue to flower the rest of the summer.

Ramblers are vigorous growers, producing long thin stems that are relatively easy to bend. Ramblers usually have small flowers in showy, dense clusters and tend to bloom only once a year, in early summer. Some ramblers produce attractive displays of fruit.

SITING AND CARE: Plant roses in full sun and give them moderate moisture and good drainage.

Train ramblers and climbing roses on any support to which they can be easily tied. Attach screw eyes to wooden walls or posts or drill holes into masonry and insert eye bolts for tying. Fasten the stems to the bolts with wire or green string. Weave roses in lattice, obelisks, or wrought iron. Tie them to arches and to freestanding pillars. Train a vigorous rose upright and then allow it to cascade downward. Strong-growing ramblers will tend to mound on themselves on top of an arbor, creating huge arches of blossoms. Training roses horizontally encourages the production of flower buds. Do not let the canes become too entwined on something you have to paint regularly. You'll need to take the vines down before painting.

Plant ramblers at the base of small trees and train the shoots into the canopy. The rose will seek the sun, and within a year or two, the tree will fill with blossoms. Choose a tree with light shade, such as an old, unproductive apple tree. Or plant the rose

'William Baffin' is a climbing Rosa rugosa hybrid hardy above ground well into zone 3. Here it is shown growing on a lattice fence.

The disease-resistant climber 'Joseph's Coat' produces roses that are a mix of yellow, orange, and red.

The double-flowered Lady Banks rose (Rosa banksiae 'Lutea') is vigorous and grows in gardens from zone 7 southward.

'Climbing Iceberg' is a climbing floribunda that produces masses of creamy white flowers in late spring into early summer, and repeats through much of the summer.

next to a relatively young tree and let the two grow old together. All climbers and ramblers bloom on old wood for their first flush of flowers. The repeat bloomers also produce blossoms on new growth. Some with little vigor require little pruning. Vigorous ones will benefit from winter removal of old shoots, since younger shoots will have more flowers.

Rambler roses bloom on old wood and therefore should not be severely pruned in winter. However, winter is the time to remove entire shoots where they have become crowded. Take out the oldest shoots, which will be the largest and colored brown and gray (young shoots tend to be green or red).

PESTS

Some roses are susceptible to Japanese beetles, aphids, mildew, and black spot. Others are rarely bothered by such pests. Choose those that are as pest free as possible to avoid extra work and frustration. Grow them in well ventilated areas to reduce fungal infestations. Spraying is an option, but climbers and ramblers can be large and difficult to reach. Remember that the best pest prevention is to keep your roses healthy and vigorous. The cultivars listed tend to be among the healthiest of the climbers and ramblers.

Growing roses with other plants can camouflage pest problems. Plant a clematis or honeysuckle to grow on a climbing rose to cloak mildewed leaves. Japanese beetles devour rose blossoms; the beetles will eat the leaves, too, but the damage is less noticeable when the rose is not isolated. Avoid repeat blooming-climbers since the beetles usually don't appear until midsummer when second bloom occurs.

Deer eat flower buds just as they are about to open, but they avoid old stems and leaves. Climbing and rambling roses, because they grow out of reach of deer, are a good way of having your roses and deer, too. Be sure to protect newly planted climbers with a barrier until the plant has grown out of grazing range.

RELATED SPECIES:
There are also some species roses used as climbers and ramblers. These are called "species" roses because they are naturally occurring species that have not been hybridized by humans. In areas where they are native, they scramble over other plants, usually on the edge of woods and in old, abandoned farm fields. Many of them make very attractive garden plants. Some of the best known species roses are *Rosa banksiae*, *R. canina*, *R. laevigata*, *R. multiflora*, *R. rubiginosa*, *R. setigera*, and *R. virginiana*.

'Blaze' has hot red flowers with a slight fragrance.

'New Dawn' is vigorous and blooms repeatedly through the summer. Here it has been trained against a wall as an espalier.

'Jeanne Lajoie' is a climbing miniature that bears masses of small pink flowers through summer.

'Madame Alfred Carriere' is hardy to zone 7 and produces its pinkish white flowers over a long period.

'America'; fragrant salmon flowers; hardy to zone 5

'Altissimo' with single, velvety red flowers; zone 6

'Peace' (climbing form); yellow-pink blooms; zone 5

'Compassion'; fragrant flowers followed by orange fruit; zone 5

'Dortmund' has large red flowers with a white center; zone 5

'Gloire De Dijon'; fragrant; tough enough for urban gardens; zone 6

'Golden Showers'; fragrant, semidouble flowers; zone 6

'Eden Rose'; fragrant pink and white flowers; repeat blooms; zones 5 to 9

'Sombreuil'; fragrant white flowers; zone 5

'Zephirine Droughin'; thornless stems with fragrant flowers; zone 5

'Phyllis Bide'; sweetly scented flowers that bloom all summer

'Henry Kelsey'; Explorer rose bred for extreme hardiness; zone 3

'American Pillar'; large clusters of bright pink flowers; zone 5

'Blairii No. 2'; large, double; very fragrant flowers; zone 6

'Celine Forestier'; fragrant; repeat bloomer; zone 7

'Complicata'; large single pink flowers with a white center; zone 3

'Dorothy Perkins'; a favorite old rambler; very fragrant; zone 7

'John Cabot'; extremely cold hardy; disease resistant; zone 3

'Seagull'; large clusters of white flowers with golden centers; zone 5

'Tausendschon'; thornless stems; great in the South; zone 7

Dog rose (Rosa canina); fragrant white or pink flowers followed by red-orange fruits; zone 5

Eglantine rose (Rosa rubiginosa); foliage smells like green apples; zone 5

Cherokee rose (Rosa laevigata); fragrant; pest resistant; does well in the Southwest; zone 8

Prairie rose (Rosa setigera); pink flowers fade to white; blooms later than other species roses; zone 4

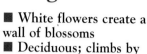

SCHIZOPHRAGMA HYDRANGEOIDES

False climbing hydrangea

■ White flowers create a wall of blossoms
■ Deciduous; climbs by rootlets
■ Once established, grows to 5 feet a year
■ Zones 6 to 8

USES: This vine looks like climbing hydrangea, and the two can be used interchangeably. It has showy white flowers and medium green leaves. Schizophragma blooms about two weeks later than climbing hydrangea, so grow them together to extend the blooming season. Or combine it with shrubby lacecap hydrangeas to repeat the lacy floral effect.

Close inspection of these two vines shows several basic differences. Hydrangea flower clusters are surrounded by four-sepaled sterile flowers; schizophragma clusters are circled with large (to 1 inch long) single bracts. Schizophragma leaves are also more coarsely toothed at the edges, the bark peels less, and in the winter the dried flower clusters droop (they are held horizontally on hydrangea). Native to Japan and Korea.

SITING AND CARE: Schizophragma grows in sun or shade. Give it moderate moisture.

Grow schizophragma on tree trunks or masonry walls, or have it trail out of containers (it is root hardy in containers outdoors to zone 6). Propagate by selecting stems already having rootlets. Cut these into 6-inch segments and bury the lower two thirds of the stems. Do this in early spring and new plants will be rooted by midsummer. False climbing hydrangea is generally pest free in the shade; Japanese beetles may attack plants growing in full sun.

RECOMMENDED CULTIVARS: 'Moonlight' was selected for gray-green foliage, which is significantly different in shape and color from the species. This foliage form is actually a juvenile trait. As the plant grows, it will eventually send out horizontal, mature shoots, with foliage a bit coarser and darker green. These shoots will produce flowers. Chinese schizophragma, *Schizophragma integrifolium*, has large (to 7 inches or more), lush leaves and larger floral bracts (each 2½ to 3½ inches wide). It is hardy in zones 7 to 9.

The white single bracts surrounding the flower clusters of false climbing hydrangea distinguish it from a true hydrangea.

SOLANUM JASMINOIDES

Potato vine

■ Showy flowers and deep green foliage
■ Scrambles; needs to be tied or woven
■ Grows 5 to 10 feet a summer
■ Zones 9 to 10; grown as an annual farther north

USES: This cousin of the true potato produces bluish white flowers. Native to Brazil.

SITING AND CARE: Grow potato vine in sun or light shade, providing moderate moisture.

Potato vine cannot climb by itself but is easily trained to scramble on and around other plants. Potato vine is usually treated as an annual, but it can be overwintered in a sunny window (watch out for whiteflies, which can be a problem indoors). Outdoors, potato beetles and whiteflies are occasional problems.

RECOMMENDED CULTIVARS: 'Album' is more commonly grown than the species. It has bright white flowers appearing continuously from midsummer until frost. It was made famous on an arch in the white garden at Sissinghurst, one of England's best-known gardens. 'Album Variegatum' has leaves with white variegation.

Solanum jasminoides 'Album' has bright white flowers that repeat bloom throughout the growing season.

Solanum dulcamara 'Variegata' has variegated leaves and purple flowers. All parts of this plant are poisonous.

STEPHANOTIS FLORIBUNDA

Madagascar jasmine

- Glossy evergreen foliage and fragrant, waxen blooms
- Evergreen; twining
- Grows 5 to 10 feet a year
- Zones 10 to 11 (tropical); or use as an annual farther north

USES: If you are looking for fragrance, this is your plant. Cut flowers are used in bridal bouquets and Hawaiian leis. The white flowers contrast strongly with the dark evergreen leaves. Keep it in a pot that you can move indoors for the winter, and during the summer have it join you on the deck, patio, or balcony. Native to Madagascar.

SITING AND CARE: Grow stephanotis in sun or partial shade. Provide moderate moisture and good drainage. To overwinter, reduce water and do not fertilize. Keep the plant in as sunny a spot as possible, but don't expect it to bloom. Summer is its time to shine. Scale and mealybug can be problems, especially indoors.

Move stephanotis outside for the summer and enjoy it indoors for the winter.

THUNBERGIA ALATA

Black-eyed Susan vine

- Bright yellow-orange flowers with brown centers
- Climbs by twining
- Grows to 6 to 8 feet
- Tropical perennial; grown as an annual

USES: These orange flowers with dark brown centers resemble black-eyed susans. The vine is easy to grow from seed and blooms from midsummer on. Native to tropical Africa.

SITING AND CARE: Grow this vine from seed in sun or partial shade and provide moderate moisture.

Use it in hanging baskets and in patio containers. Try planting this climber on bamboo tripods amidst actual black-eyed susans (*Rudbeckia*), allowing it to rise above the other flowers.

RECOMMENDED CULTIVARS: Cultivars include 'Alba' and 'Bakeri', both with white flowers; 'Aurantiaca', with yellowish orange blossoms; and 'Susy Mixed', a mix of flower colors ranging from orange to yellow to white.

The Bengal clock vine (*Thunbergia grandiflora*) has blue flowers with yellow throats, set against leaves reaching 8 inches in length. Grow this tropical as an annual in partial shade for blooms from mid-summer until cold weather. Overwinter it indoors or let it die with the first frost.

The orange and brown flowers of Susy black-eyed Susan vine.

TRACHELOSPERMUM JASMINOIDES

Confederate jasmine, Star jasmine

- A dense evergreen with fragrant flowers
- Evergreen; climbs by twining
- Vigorous; grows to 15 feet or more
- Zones 8 to 10

USES: Plant this one for your nose. Creamy white tubular flowers are star shaped with an intense fragrance in late spring and early summer. Plant jasmine near a patio or anywhere you will enjoy it in the evening, when the flowers stand out due to their whiteness and fragrance. It is generally little troubled by pests. Native to China.

SITING AND CARE: This vine does best in shade but will tolerate light sun. Provide moderate moisture with good drainage.

Plant it on trellises, lattice, or chain link fences. Use confederate jasmine in a pot, trained on a cage of green mesh. This climber also serves as a ground cover and will blanket slopes.

RECOMMENDED CULTIVARS: 'Japonicum' has leaves with white veins; its foliage turns bronze in autumn and winter. 'Minimum' has mottled leaves and a dwarf habit.

Confederate jasmine produces masses of fragrant flowers.

Nasturtium cultivars. Top, 'Hermine Grashoff'; center, a double form; bottom, 'Alaska'.

Nasturtium flowers and leaves are beautiful and edible.

TROPAEOLUM MAJUS

Nasturtium

- Fragrant, edible, brightly colored flowers throughout the summer
- Scrambles; climbs by twisting leaf stalks
- Grows to 8 feet
- Annual; good for areas with cool summers

USES: This attractive annual has edible yellow, orange, or red flowers appearing all summer until frost. The leaves are round and attached at the center like parasols. Both leaves and flowers taste peppery and add visual and culinary spice to salads. The buds are sometimes pickled and used as caper substitutes. This vine is perfect for children's gardens because all parts of the plants are edible. Nasturtium grows best with cool summers and loses vigor in hot, dry summers. The French impressionist painter Monet used nasturtiums in his garden at Giverny as a groundcover beneath arches of climbing roses. Let it climb over a yew hedge or scramble amidst purple leaves and flowers. Native to Columbia and Bolivia.

SITING AND CARE: Grow nasturtium in full sun to partial shade. Give it moderate moisture. Plant seeds directly in the garden after danger of frost has passed. Root extra plants from young shoots (they'll root in water or in potting soil).

Use nasturtium on trellises, netting, or sprawling over plants. It is not overly vigorous and is easily kept in control in a pot or hanging basket. Aphids and other insects are occasional problems.

RECOMMENDED CULTIVARS: Hybrids include the Florepleno Series, with double flowers; and Climbing Hybrids Improved, with a wide range of colors. The cultivar 'Variegatus' has leaves splashed with white and flowers of orange and red. Avoid the dwarf selections if you want a vine.

Canary creeper has showy, bright yellow fringed flowers repeating throughout the summer.

TROPAEOLUM PEREGRINUM

Canary creeper

- Showy, bright yellow fringed flowers repeating throughout the summer
- Scrambles; leafstalks twist around supports
- Grows up to 10 feet tall
- Annual; good for areas with cool summers

USES: The fringed flowers do indeed look as if miniature canaries were perched on its stems. Although in the same genus as nasturtium, the two vines look very different. However, canary creeper also has edible, peppery-tasting leaves and flowers. Canary creeper leaves are distinctly lobed and up to 3 inches across. Native to Peru and Ecuador.

SITING AND CARE: Grow in full sun to partial shade. It prefers cool summers and tends to do poorly when the weather becomes hot. Provide extra water when the weather turns dry. Sow the seeds directly in the garden after all danger of frost has passed. Plants are intolerant of any frost and will die in the fall. Use canary creeper as a ground cover, allow it to scramble over a large shrub, or train it up lattice or netting. It is outstanding in a pot or a hanging basket.

VITIS COIGNETIAE

Crimson glory vine

- Bold leaves with great fall color
- Deciduous; climbs by tendrils
- Very vigorous; grows up to 20 feet a season
- Zones 5 to 9

USES: The bold leaves of this ornamental grape reach 10 inches across. Rusty brown hairs cover the undersides of the leaves, which turn brilliant orange-red in autumn. The small green flowers are hidden by the foliage and are followed by inedible, blue-black fruits. Take advantage of its bold foliage. Use it with other large-leaved plants, such as oakleaf hydrangea, or contrast it with the fine textures of pines or spireas. The fall color will be best in full sun. Combine crimson glory vine with late-summer purple flowers such as aster and joe-pye weed, as well as with the red-orange fruits of crabapples and roses. Native to Japan and Korea.

SITING AND CARE: Grow in sun or light shade. Provide moderate moisture and good drainage.

Cover chain link and large arbors with this fast-growing vine. Give it lots of space or prune it each summer. Since it is not grown for fruit or flowers, timing of pruning doesn't matter. This is a good espalier plant because it recovers from pruning mistakes quickly. Mildew and Japanese beetles can be problems. Wasps may be attracted to ripe fruit.

RELATED SPECIES: The common grape, *Vitis vinifera*, is the wine grape. Hardy to zones 6 to 9, it is usually only grown for grape production. The cultivar 'Purpurea', however, is ornamental. Its hairy, deeply lobed leaves emerge green but soon turn purplish. The cooler the climate, the deeper the purple. The leaves need full sun to color well. Its fruit is not especially tasty.

Edible grapes are in the same genus, *Vitis*. They, too, can be used ornamentally for their bold leaves. Fruit, used for desserts and wine production, is produced on short spur shoots that form along the stem. Prune in winter, cutting shoots back to four to six spurs per stem. Prune further in midsummer to remove excessively long shoots. Japanese beetles are especially fond of any grape leaf growing in full sun, and can virtually defoliate vines.

Autumn turns the foliage of ornamental grapes brilliant colors. Crimson glory vine is at left; purple-leafed wine grape at right.

'Brant' is a hybrid grape. Its deciduous leaves (except for the veins) turn bronze-red in autumn.

Crimson glory vine leaves are a quiet gray-green in summer and turn brilliant red in fall. The fruit is not edible.

The leaves of purple-leafed wine grape are more lobed than those of crimson glory vine, and are a blend of purple and green during summer. Here, it is growing with wisteria.

WISTERIA FLORIBUNDA

Japanese wisteria

- Impressively long clusters of fragrant purple flowers in midspring
- Deciduous; climbs by twining
- Vigorous; grows up to 15 feet a year
- Southern part of zones 5 to 9

USES: This Japanese native in full bloom is a memorable sight. It is one of the most beautiful of flowering vines, yet it can also be most challenging due to its vigor and strength. This is not a climber for weakly made structures. Many an arbor has collapsed under the twisting weight of wisteria.

The fragrant flowers are bluish violet, with cultivars varying from purple to pink to white. Individually small (less than an inch in length), the flowers are borne in pendant clusters from 8 to 24 inches long (the longer the better). The flowers open gradually, from the base of the cluster to the tip. The first flowers open just as the leaves are unfolding, and by the time the last flower bud opens, the plant is in full leaf. The inedible fruits are thick, velvety green, 6 inch-long pods that resemble beans.

The foot-long leaves have 11 to 19 leaflets, each about 3 inches long. They are unmarred by insects or diseases and form a dense screen throughout the summer. They turn pale yellow before dropping in autumn. The smooth, gray trunks become picturesque with age, sinuously wrapping around themselves. The trunk and leaf buds survive zone 4 winters, but the flower buds do not. Native to Japan.

SITING AND CARE: Japanese wisteria needs full sun and moderate moisture for good flowering.

Plant it on wrought iron and on large arbors and arches. This vine should only be planted on strong, maintenance-free structures; it will live decades, and painting or rebuilding the structure will be difficult.

The Asian species of wisteria are spectacular, displaying their flowers just before the leaves emerge.

This white cultivar of Japanese wisteria has long, graceful clusters of flowers.

Getting a new wisteria to bloom can be a challenge, often requiring a wait of 5 to 10 years. Root pruning, withholding irrigation, and using only phosphate fertilizer (absolutely no nitrogen) may bring a reluctant wisteria into bloom. Seedlings seem to be especially slow to bloom and there may be an advantage to buying a plant already of blooming age. Wisterias require frequent pruning to keep them within desired boundaries. Blossoms occur on spur shoots, which are short side shoots off the main stems. Avoid removing them when pruning. Do major pruning right after flowering ends, plus one or two midsummer prunings of long shoots, cutting them back to the main part of the plant. In winter, do additional pruning to shape the plant, but avoid removing the spur shoots. Old wisteria stems (living or dead) make very attractive supports for other vines.

RECOMMENDED CULTIVARS: Two of the best cultivars are 'Macrobotrys' (also known as 'Longissima' and 'Multijuga'), with extremely long (to 36 inches) clusters of lavender-blue flowers; and 'Longissima Alba', with white flower clusters only a bit shorter (to 24 inches). Other cultivars include 'Alba'

Japanese wisteria typically has long, somewhat open clusters of flowers, and the individual flowers gradually open from the top down. This cultivar, 'Violacea Plena', has double flowers.

and 'Issai Perfect', both with white flower clusters to 14 inches; 'Issai', bluish flowers in clusters 24 to 32 inches long; 'Rosea', with pink flowers in 18 inch-long clusters; 'Royal Purple', deep violet flowers in 12 inch-long clusters; and 'Violacea-Plena', purplish double flowers in clusters up to 12 inches long.

Chinese wisteria, *Wisteria sinensis*, is a similar species and difficult to distinguish from Japanese wisteria except when in bloom. Chinese wisteria flowers appear before the leaves, in smaller clusters (6 to 12 inches long), and with the fragrant blossoms opening all at once. It is hardy to zones 6 to 9 and generally has blue-violet flowers. 'Alba' is white; 'Jako' is also white, but with longer flower clusters; 'Amethyst' has rosy-purple flower clusters, 'Aunt Dee' has 12-inch lavender clusters; 'Black Dragon' has purple semidouble flowers; 'Blue' has lavender-blue flowers; 'Plena' has lavender double flowers; 'Sierra Madre' has bicolored white-and-lavender blossoms; and 'Rosea' is pink.

Kentucky wisteria, *W. macrostachya*, is a native American species occurring in the southern Midwest. It is not as vigorous as the above species and is easier to use in most gardens. Its flowers appear after the leaves (two to three weeks after the Asians) but are still quite showy. Hardy in zones 5 to 9, it has lilac-colored flowers in 8 inch-long clusters. 'Abbeville Blue' has pale blue flowers while 'Pondside Blue' is a deeper blue with very dense flower clusters. 'Clara Mack' has white flowers in clusters 10 to 14 inches long.

Wisterias, with help from extremely strong stakes and lots of pruning, can be trained into tree forms. These Japanese wisteria "trees" at Longwood Gardens display their flowers between the horizontal branches and shimmer in the wind like dancing petticoats.

American wisteria, *W. frutescens*, is native to the southeastern United States. Its flower clusters resemble inverted cones and are only 4 inches long, occurring well after the leaves are out. The lavender to purple blossoms combine beautifully with yellows and oranges. Try *Wisteria frutescens* with *Lonicera flava*. This wisteria grows much less vigorously than the Asian species and is easier to keep within bounds. 'Magnifica' has lilac flowers with a yellow blotch in the center; 'Nivea' has white flowers. Hardy in zones 6 to 9.

With multiple prunings throughout the year, wisteria can be grown in a container and kept within bounds in even a small garden.

The white flowers of Wisteria frutescens 'Alba' appear after the leaves emerge. American wisteria is not as vigorous as the Asian species and is easier to use in most gardens.

The lavender blossoms of American wisteria are not as breathtaking as those of its Asian cousins, but the plant is beautiful nonetheless.

THE USDA PLANT HARDINESS ZONE MAP OF NORTH AMERICA

Plants are classified according to the amount of cold weather they can handle. For example, a plant listed as hardy to zone 6 will survive a winter in which the temperature drops to minus 10° F.

Warm weather also influences whether a plant will survive in your region. Although this map does not address heat hardiness, in general, if a range of hardiness zones are listed for a plant, the plant will survive winter in the coldest zone as well as tolerate the heat of the warmest zone.

To use this map, find the location of your community, then match the color band marking that area to the zone key below.

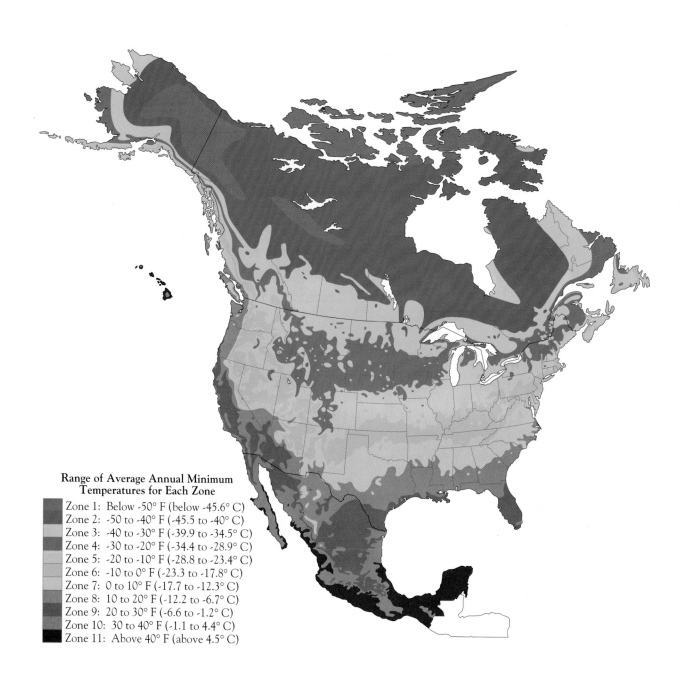

Range of Average Annual Minimum Temperatures for Each Zone

Zone 1: Below -50° F (below -45.6° C)
Zone 2: -50 to -40° F (-45.5 to -40° C)
Zone 3: -40 to -30° F (-39.9 to -34.5° C)
Zone 4: -30 to -20° F (-34.4 to -28.9° C)
Zone 5: -20 to -10° F (-28.8 to -23.4° C)
Zone 6: -10 to 0° F (-23.3 to -17.8° C)
Zone 7: 0 to 10° F (-17.7 to -12.3° C)
Zone 8: 10 to 20° F (-12.2 to -6.7° C)
Zone 9: 20 to 30° F (-6.6 to -1.2° C)
Zone 10: 30 to 40° F (-1.1 to 4.4° C)
Zone 11: Above 40° F (above 4.5° C)

INDEX

Numbers in italics denote photographs or illustrations. Boldface numbers refer to lead entries in the "Selection and Growing Guide."

METRIC CONVERSIONS

U.S. Units to Metric Equivalents			Metric Units to U.S. Equivalents		
To Convert From	Multiply By	To Get	To Convert From	Multiply By	To Get
Inches	25.4	Millimetres	Millimetres	0.0394	Inches
Inches	2.54	Centimetres	Centimetres	0.3937	Inches
Feet	30.48	Centimetres	Centimetres	0.0328	Feet
Feet	0.3048	Metres	Metres	3.2808	Feet
Yards	0.9144	Metres	Metres	1.0936	Yards
Square inches	6.4516	Square centimetres	Square centimetres	0.1550	Square inches
Square feet	0.0929	Square metres	Square metres	10.764	Square feet
Square yards	0.8361	Square metres	Square metres	1.1960	Square yards
Acres	0.4047	Hectares	Hectares	2.4711	Acres
Cubic inches	16.387	Cubic centimetres	Cubic centimetres	0.0610	Cubic inches
Cubic feet	0.0283	Cubic metres	Cubic metres	35.315	Cubic feet
Cubic feet	28.316	Litres	Litres	0.0353	Cubic feet
Cubic yards	0.7646	Cubic metres	Cubic metres	1.308	Cubic yards
Cubic yards	764.55	Litres	Litres	0.0013	Cubic yards

To convert from degrees Fahrenheit (F) to degrees Celsius (C), first subtract 32, then multiply by ⁵⁄₉.

To convert from degrees Celsius to degrees Fahrenheit, multiply by ⁹⁄₅, then add 32.